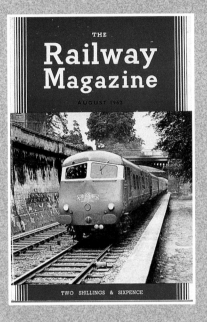

THE
Railway
Magazine

AUGUST 1962

TWO SHILLINGS & SIXPENCE

THE
RAILWAY MAGAZINE

JULY
1983
2/6

THE BUNTINGFORD
RAILWAY
Centenary of the Great Eastern singleline
branch from St. Margarets to Buntingford

LANDORE DIESEL DEPOT
A further step in the Western Region
dieselisation plan in South Wales

MUSEUM OF BRITISH
TRANSPORT
Opening of main section of rail and road
museum at Clapham, London

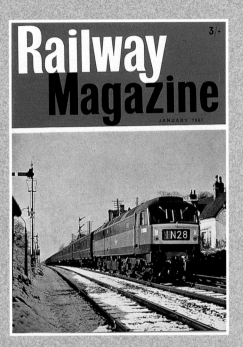

3/-

Railway
Magazine

JANUARY 1967

55p

Railway
Magazine

OCTOBER 1980

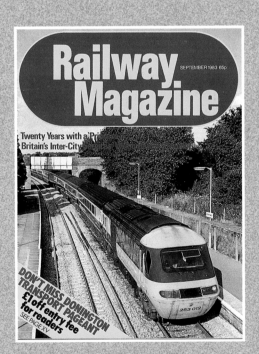

Railway
Magazine

SEPTEMBER 1983 65p

Twenty Years with a 'Pr
Britain's Inter-City

DON'T MISS DONINGTON
TRANSPORT PAGEANT
£1 off entry fee
for readers
SEE PAGE XV

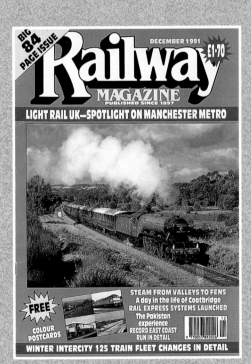

BIG
84
PAGE ISSUE

DECEMBER 1991

Railway
MAGAZINE
PUBLISHED SINCE 1897

£1·70

LIGHT RAIL UK—SPOTLIGHT ON MANCHESTER METRO

FREE
COLOUR
POSTCARDS

STEAM FROM VALLEYS TO FENS
A day in the life of Coatbridge
RAIL EXPRESS SYSTEMS LAUNCHED
The Pakistan
experience
RECORD EAST COAST
RUN IN DETAIL

WINTER INTERCITY 125 TRAIN FLEET CHANGES IN DETAIL

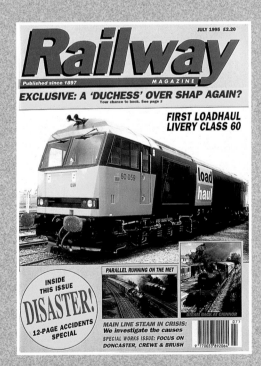

JULY 1995 £2.20

Railway
MAGAZINE
Published since 1897

EXCLUSIVE: A 'DUCHESS' OVER SHAP AGAIN?
Your chance to book. See page 3

FIRST LOADHAUL
LIVERY CLASS 60

INSIDE
THIS ISSUE
DISASTER!
12-PAGE ACCIDENTS
SPECIAL

PARALLEL RUNNING ON THE MET

MAIN LINE STEAM IN CRISIS:
We investigate the causes
SPECIAL WORKS ISSUE: FOCUS ON
DONCASTER, CREWE & BRUSH

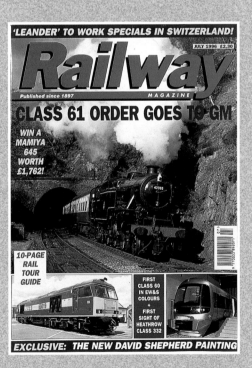

'LEANDER' TO WORK SPECIALS IN SWITZERLAND!

JULY 1996 £2.30

Railway
MAGAZINE
Published since 1897

CLASS 61 ORDER GOES TO GM

WIN A
MAMIYA
645
WORTH
£1,762!

10-PAGE
RAIL
TOUR
GUIDE

FIRST
CLASS 60
IN EW&S
COLOURS

FIRST
SIGHT OF
HEATHROW
CLASS 332

EXCLUSIVE: THE NEW DAVID SHEPHERD PAINTING

A Century of
RAILWAYS

*An appropriately-named locomotive – the LNER's Gresley
Pacific No. 2555* Centenary. *It was the first engine built by
Doncaster Works in 1925, the year of the Railway
Centenary celebrations. (See Chapter 2).* NRM

A Century of
RAILWAYS

Through the pages of 'Railway Magazine' and
paintings from members of the Guild of Railway Artists

INCLUDES THE 100-YEAR HISTORY OF 'RAILWAY MAGAZINE',

by Peter W. B. Semmens

Foreword by HRH The Duke of Gloucester

Oxford Publishing Co.

First published in 1996.

A catalogue record for this book is available from the
British Library.

ISBN 0-86093-535-3

Library of Congress Catalog Card No. 96-75829

Oxford Publishing Co. is an imprint of Haynes Publishing,
Sparkford, Nr Yeovil, Somerset BA22 7JJ

Printed in Hong Kong

Typeset in Times Roman Medium

As part of our ongoing market research, we are always
pleased to receive comments about our books, suggestions
for new titles, or requests for catalogues. Please write to:
The Editorial Director, Oxford Publishing Co., Sparkford,
Nr Yeovil, Somerset, BA22 7JJ

FOREWORD

KENSINGTON PALACE
LONDON W8 4PU

No history of the British would be complete without reference to the way a steam railway system was able to boost the industrialization of the country by linking all parts of it together, a system exported to many colonies around the world thus creating an economic force of Imperial dimensions.

Steam has been supplanted at the same time as that Empire, but not in the affections of many people, who enjoyed the splendour with which the giant machines filled our eyes with gleaming metal, our ears with the throb of raw power and our noses with that mixture of smoke and steam that is so evocative.

Photographs can portray the lines and outline of this phenomena, but the more skilled of painters can encapsulate the effect of many tons of metal propelled at great speed through all kinds of weather and light, emitting the variations of smoke and steam that have to be just so to reveal the true character of the engine.

Railway Magazine has a depth of experience to understand the contribution that artists have made to our image of Railways and, in creating the memorial to their achievements, they are celebrating not only their own centenary but also the enthusiasm of those who know, not only how to evaluate an engine, but how to record its moods in paint.

The large numbers of people involved in Railway Preservation and Restoration bears witness that Railways are not just a transport system, and Railway Magazine has existed for a hundred years on the basis that a large portion of the public want to know a lot more about the system, past, present and future, than what happens to meet the eye of the traveller.

I hope this history of the Magazine, and the paintings chosen to illustrate it, will reveal to both enthusiasts and the uninformed how a mere mechanical system can inspire such interest and delight in those who appreciate it.

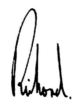

HRH The Duke of Gloucester

CONTENTS

Foreword by HRH The Duke of Gloucester   4

Introduction by Nick Pigott, Editor, *Railway Magazine*   6

The Story of *Railway Magazine*   7

A Century of Major Railway Events
  Seen Through the Columns of *Railway Magazine*   15

The Changing Enthusiast Scene   31

A Celebration in Art by the Guild of Railway Artists   33

The Railway Magazine *was launched in the summer of
1897, the year of Queen Victoria's Diamond Jubilee. On
14th June that year, the London & North Western Railway
turned out Webb 'Greater Britain' class 2-2-2-2 compound
No. 2054* Queen Empress *in a remarkable lavender and
cream livery with brass boiler bands and white tyres, to
celebrate the royal occasion.* NRM

INTRODUCTION

'*Railway Magazine* is more than a periodical. It is very nearly a national institution.'

It was with those words that I introduced my first column as editor of Britain's senior railway publication – and as we celebrate our centenary, those sentiments are, I feel, more appropriate than ever.

For the past 100 years, *Railway Magazine* has been synonymous with railways themselves. It has chronicled their achievements, predicted their fortunes, celebrated their triumphs and chastised their failings, while all the time faithfully and comprehensively monitoring the enormous changes that have taken place during that era.

It is perhaps hard to believe that when our first issue came off the press, much of the Great Central Railway was still under construction, that an entire quarter of a century was to elapse before anyone would even hear of the LNER or the LMS, that both world wars still lay in the distant future – and that the vast majority of today's preserved steam locomotives were still figments of draughtsmen's imaginations!

In fact, it sometimes seems that the only thing that hasn't changed over that period is the distance between the rails! Yet as far as the centenarians of our society are concerned, all these events have occurred within a human lifetime – a fact which merely serves to underline the sheer pace of change on our nation's railways since 1897.

The task of keeping abreast of those developments and recording them for posterity is the one which has been set the editorial teams over the decades. For the seven men who have borne the title of Editor, there have been some particularly heavy crosses to bear. For G. A. Sekon, it was the risk of launching a totally new and untried product onto a market still largely unaccustomed to the idea of periodical purchasing. To John Gairns, William Willox and John Kay fell the task of steering the title through the rigours and restraints of global conflicts. Gairns also had to contend with the 1923 grouping and Kay with nationalisation, while the present editorial team and myself have had to wrestle with the astonishingly complex and amorphous world of privatisation.

We certainly provide today's reader with far more knowledge in the form of news stories and news pictures than was ever the case in the past. Immense pride is taken in the fact that ours is the only title exhaustively covering the entire British contemporary and steam railway spectrum from A to Z with overseas interest thrown in.

As a journal of record, *Railway Magazine* has few peers and with its 100 years of indices, has built up into the most comprehensive and definitive register of British railway history. However, 1,150 or so issues are more than just a little unwieldy and beyond both the shelf space and pocket of the average enthusiast or historian. Hence the publication of this book.

We wished, in a nutshell, to encapsulate the major events of the century in a readily-digestible form and to tell, for the first time ever, the full history of *Railway Magazine* itself.

It was without hesitation that I invited our Chief Correspondent, Peter Semmens, to undertake the research and authorship of this prestigious project. Peter has been associated with the magazine for many years and has been the compiler of our famous 'Practice & Performance' series (the longest-running railway column in the world) since January 1981.

His lifelong interest in railways has taken him all over the world and there are very few types of train he has not either travelled upon or footplated. Few people are better qualified to compile the text of such a wide-ranging subject.

To illustrate the editorial, we have drawn mainly from our own extensive photo-archives, with help from other sources such as the collection of the National Railway Museum.

But, as will quickly become apparent, this is no mere book of text and photographs. As befits an occasion as illustrious as the centenary of *Railway Magazine*, we have joined forces with the esteemed Guild of Railway Artists to produce a sumptuous 'coffee table book' relating the story of the century in glorious colour.

Each artist has been invited to put forward a selection of paintings representing scenes or events from the past 100 years. Some have chosen historical subjects, others more recent scenes, but together they build up into a broadly representative overview of the century, depicting many scenes it would otherwise have been impossible to illustrate in colour.

We believe this book is the perfect companion for all regular readers of *Railway Magazine* and all lovers of fine art and that it will become a valuable work of reference for those seeking to study the railways of the 20th century and the history of railway publishing.

Here's to the next 100 years!

Nick Pigott
Editor, *Railway Magazine*

THE STORY OF *RAILWAY MAGAZINE*

THE LAUNCH

The mechanisation of printing, like the railways, was a product of the Industrial Revolution, so it was not surprising that a railway publication – *Herepath's Railway Magazine* – should make its appearance as early as 1835. That was basically about railway finance, as was *Bradshaw's Railway Manual, Shareholders' Guide and Official Directory*, which appeared with slight variations in title from 1848 until 1923, when the Grouping made it superfluous. Much better known, and more widely used, was *Bradshaw's Guide*, first published in 1841, which, until its demise in 1961, gave the times of passenger trains throughout the British Isles.

As the 1800s drew to a close, this country's railways were changing rapidly as they built up towards the zenith of their influence and prosperity during the first decade of the 20th century. The railways were employing increasingly larger numbers of staff and, in the days before Workmen's Compensation Acts were fully effective, there were several private opportunities for employees to take out some sort of personal cover. One such scheme was run by Joseph Lawrence's Railway Publishing Company. Anyone with a pre-paid subscription to its weekly *Railway Herald* – a publication aimed mainly at railwaymen – was covered by a special insurance policy.

As prosperity in the country increased, more comforts were demanded by railway passengers. One only has to visit the National Railway Museum and compare the Midland six-wheel 'composite' of 1885 with the London & North Western's first-class diner of 15 years later to appreciate how rapid were the changes. Journeys by rail had ceased to be trials of fortitude, and people were beginning to travel for pleasure, and enjoy the experience.

The public's reactions to the 1895 'Races to the North' demonstrated another form of interest. Late at night, after the locomotive change in Newcastle, it was reported that 'amid enthusiastic cheers and waving of handkerchiefs the next stage of the journey was resumed'. In addition, there were the stalwarts who dashed backwards and forwards between London and Aberdeen, recording the times and speeds at first hand, apparently at some considerable risk to life and limb. Approaching Edinburgh, the North Eastern 4-4-0 No. 1691, now preserved in the National

Railway Museum, took the reverse curves at Portobello at more than 80mph instead of the usual 15. After the group of timekeepers had picked themselves up off the floor, one of them remarked, 'We would have made bonnie raspberry jam in that Duddingston Road'.

There was thus a growing popular interest in railways, their equipment, and their methods of operation, and in January 1886, *Moore's Monthly Magazine* began to appear. This was intended initially as an adjunct to the sale of F. Moore's locomotive photographs, but after a year, a more descriptive title *The Locomotive Magazine* was adopted, the magazine continuing to be published until 1959.

Frank Cornwall was the Manager of the *Railway Herald*, having previously worked on the Manchester, Sheffield & Lincolnshire, and Cape Government railways, and he developed the idea of producing a railway publication of 'general interest' for Joseph Lawrence's company. Initially he was thinking of an annual – *The Railway Year Book* – but after getting one of his *Railway Herald* contributors, George Augustus Nokes, to start compiling it, the idea was changed to a monthly magazine. In 1885/86 they had published *Railway Herald Magazine* as a 'penny monthly', and just dropped the word 'Herald' from the title. After raising the necessary capital, Cornwall invited Nokes – who, as described below, more usually used the pseudonym Sekon – to become the first Editor of *The Railway Magazine*. The first issue appeared in July 1897, price 6 pence (2½p), and consisted of 96 pages, 6¾in by 9½in. Many half-tone blocks were included, in addition to the line-drawings, which, up to then, were the more traditional means of reproducing illustrations.

The magazine began with an 'Illustrated Interview' with a senior railway manager, a feature that was to appear for a number of years. The first railway officer involved was Mr Joseph Loftus Wilkinson, the General Manager of the Great Western. As Nokes recounted in our Jubilee issue for July/August 1947, he had written a book, *History of the Great Western Railway – the Story of the Broad Gauge*, in 1895, and dedicated it to F. G. Saunders, the then Chairman of that company. This prompted him to approach Wilkinson about the idea of the interview, but it was not easy to convince him that it would 'arouse such interest that it would be the most popular and important descriptive of a railway and railway working ever published'. However, he eventually agreed, and the article was written.

Sekon used the 'question and answer' format,

which enabled the interviewee to list his railway's improvements over the years. The editor concluded with a question about the new magazine, and Wilkinson's reply was, 'There is, in my judgement, an excellent opening for such a magazine. If worked with enterprise and vigour, and kept absolutely neutral, as between the various railway companies, it will be subscribed to by many railwaymen and those connected with them'. One could hardly wish for a better recommendation! Nokes was right about the importance of the interview, and not only did the series continue, but Wilkinson himself contributed an article, 'The General Manager', six months later.

The next article in the first issue covered 'Fifty Years of Railway Engineering' and was an account of the career of Richard Johnson, who had just retired as Chief Engineer of the Great Northern Railway. One of the structures described was the 'New Copenhagen Tunnel' outside King's Cross, which, in spite of today's vastly-increased number of trains, has been disused since the station's 'throat' was remodelled in 1977 ready for the introduction of the HSTs.

This was followed with a contribution by

Charles Rous-Marten, 'Recent Work by British Express Locomotives', the forerunner of his 1901 'Practice & Performance' series which will be described later. Then came V. L. Whitechurch's 'The Slip Coach Mystery – A Railway Adventure', which was a typical 'gung-ho' yarn of the period, with the hero at one point working his way along the footboards of the moving train to thwart the machinations of a mysterious East European.

Next came the first part of the Rev. W. J. Scott's series, 'Some "Racing Runs" and Trial Trips', dealing with the last day of the races to Edinburgh in 1888, when he travelled on the 10am from King's Cross. The brief, ten-word caption to an illustration that accompanied it, showing a Stirling 'Single' on the outskirts of London, became the first classic quote from the magazine, 'We came finely up the long bank to Potter's Bar'.

Another first-hand account of a railway journey followed, this time by Herbert Russell, who had travelled on the footplate of *Courier*, a Dean 4-2-2, hauling 'The Flying Welshman' from Newport to Paddington. Approaching the Severn Tunnel, he commented to driver George Evans that 'Many people consider the Severn Tunnel as dangerous. What do you think?'. The reply was, 'Well, I suppose their notion is that there's a certain amount of risk in going under the water, but if you ask me my honest opinion, I don't see why the Severn Tunnel shouldn't be quite as safe as any other'. A century later one wonders how many rail passengers between England and Wales now actually notice the Severn Tunnel as they pass through it. Nevertheless there are those who are apprehensive of going through the Channel Tunnel, although the water leakage along its vastly-greater underwater length is probably not all that much more than the daily quantities that are still pumped out of the Severn Tunnel.

In 1897 the big railway project of the time was the construction of the Great Central Railway, and that formed the subject for the next article in issue No. 1. A map of the route was included among the illustrations, being a *sine qua non* for any self-respecting article about a new railway line. Herbert Russell's second contribution followed, giving a description of the new Royal Train built for Queen Victoria's Diamond Jubilee by the Great Western Railway. He had been shown over it by William Dean, who drew his attention to the 'exquisitely painted design of the Imperial insignia' on its exterior, which had been 'executed by a man over seventy-two years of age'. It is an interesting thought that the craftsman concerned would have been born in the year that the Stockton & Darlington Railway opened. Two technical articles followed, describing the 'Vacuum Automatic Brake' and the 'Independent Rail Joint'.

In 1897 the magazine's layout was somewhat different to what later became the norm, and empty spaces at the ends of articles, sometimes more than half a page high, were filled with line-drawings. The printer clearly had not had time to develop any with an appropriate railway theme, and the rail joint article was rounded off with a reclining Cupid, although he is about to make a note in a book, so maybe was writing up the day's list of locomotives he had 'spotted'.

The last major article in our first issue was on 'Railway Finance', by W. J. Stevens, 'Author of *Home Railways as Investments*. It was announced as a monthly series, with sections covering the Stock Market, as well as British, American, Colonial and foreign railways, with 'Notes on Railway Finance'.

After the stock-market review came another regular early series, 'What the Railways are Doing', the forerunner of 'Notes & News' that, in turn, ran for well over half a century. Language in 1897 was much more flowery than we are used to, and many of the items seem to be based somewhat uncritically on railway advertisements or other publications. The 'North Eastern' entry read as follows:

'What can be done without competition? A glance at the full and novel arrangements of the NER clearly shows that competition is not needed to cause the General Manager of that Company to provide in a most generous spirit all reasonable facilities for both business and pleasure travellers over the splendid system. Several portions of the NER are now celebrating their jubilees.'

In fact there were times when the NER's territorial monopoly caused considerable adverse local comment in the area it served!

The section 'Pertinent Paragraphs' followed, and again appeared for many years. Reading the entries during the writing of this book was quite an amusing activity, as some dealt with remarkably trivial subjects, while others recounted classic 'chestnuts' from the contemporary press. In some cases one can also come across an entry that is still pertinent today, such as the second paragraph in our first issue. This read:

'Now anyone with the slightest acquaintance with the London railway termini knows that the Midland terminus at St. Pancras can accommodate a great deal more traffic than it does at present.'

The concern today is how soon the Eurostars and high-speed commuter trains will start to use the station after the completion of the Channel Tunnel Rail Link.

Our first issue concluded on Page 96, with 'Railway Patents – The Inventor's Opportunity'. In it, readers were told that a letter to '"The Patent Editor, Railway Magazine, 16, Serjeants' Inn, Fleet Street, E.C.," will be the first step towards obtaining the assistance and advice the inventor requires'. The average inventor has rarely made a fortune, and those coming up with railway improvements have perhaps fared even worse than most, as most companies had an almost pathological dislike of using patents held by outsiders.

Looking back nearly a century, one can but admire the content of our first issue, and the editor of a new railway magazine in the 1990s would be hard-pushed to better the appeal and scope of the 1897 material used by Nokes. It is not surprising that *Railway Magazine* flourished under his editorship, and this led to grandiose plans to produce other magazines from the Serjeants' Inn address, including titles such as *Army & Navy Magazine Illustrated*, and *Public Schools Magazine Illustrated*, but nothing came of them. The premises were never actually occupied and only used briefly for the delivery of correspondence, before a move was made to 79/80, Temple Chambers, Temple Avenue, E.C.

Jumping forward two years, several of the items featured in the first issue were still appearing, although the Stock Market reports had ceased. The 'Illustrated Interview' still had pride of place at the front, while 'What the Railways are Doing' and 'Pertinent Paragraphs' brought up the rear. As appropriate for a summer issue, most of the July 1899 one was devoted to railway

A scene from the very month of the magazine's launch – July 1897 – depicting Great Northern Railway Stirling 8ft Single No. 98 pausing at Finsbury Park.

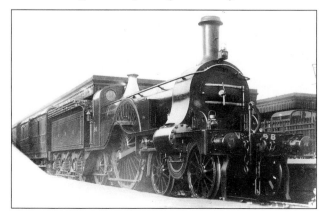

journeys to tourist areas, such as the North Cornwall Coast, Jersey, and even Grimsby and Cleethorpes ('The Great Central Railway's Port and Seaside Resort'). Skegness had not yet invented its 'Jolly Fisherman' with which to trump the latter town! Articles on overseas railways had started to appear, Northern India featuring in the November issue, and the Danish State Railways in the September one.

EDITORS AND OWNERS

The roles of owner and editor are vital for any magazine. It is the former's decisions that determine whether it will appear on the news-stands, but the editor has the day-to-day task of producing it, and is the person whom the readership primarily identifies as being responsible for its production and contents. It is therefore convenient to review the first century of *Railway Magazine's* progress by combining information about each of the editors with an outline of the changes in content and the ownership of the title that took place during their tenure of office.

1897-1910

Reference has already been made to George Augustus Nokes (1867-1948). He lived in Thanet during his early years, where he developed a childhood interest in railway operation. To begin with he was attracted to the London, Chatham & Dover Railway, but later extended his visits to its fiercely-competitive rival, the South Eastern Railway. After education at Hayes Grammar School and Hayes College, he entered the surveying and land agency profession in 1885. One day he purchased a set of *The Railway Herald* being auctioned by his firm, which interested him in journalism, and began to contribute to this publication, using the pen-name G. A. Sekon – his own with the letters reversed. This was later to become better known than his proper surname, which at one time he used to sign as 'nnokes.'

As recounted earlier, when the idea of launching *Railway Magazine* was being considered by the proprietors of *Railway Herald*, they invited Nokes to become the founding editor, a post he held until 1910. He then fell out with Sir Joseph Lawrence, the owner of the Railway Publishing Company, for reasons never quite clarified, and founded a rival publication – *Railway & Travel Monthly*. Thirteen years later, under the control of John Kay, this was to be merged into *Railway Magazine*.

George Augustus Nokes
(a.k.a. G. A. Sekon)
Editor 1897-1910

Nokes died in 1948, still actively writing about railways at the age of 81. The first of his two-part article on the LBSCR East Coast Section followed the tribute to him in our May/June 1948 issue. As his obituary stated, 'His activities resulted in the eventual triumph of popular interest as a recognised and legitimate feature of railway operation, and indeed, a valuable asset'.

1910-1930

Our second Editor, John Francis Gairns (1876-1930) joined the staff of a patent agency when he was 18. By 1910 he had contributed for many years to *Railway Magazine* and *Railway News*, and was chosen to take over the editorship of the former when Nokes left. During the next two decades he not only edited the magazine, but contributed 'many comprehensive articles on practically all railway subjects'. He was also a regular contributor to *Railway News* before it was incorporated into *Railway Gazette* in 1918, and in 1924 Gairns became Assistant Editor of the latter, and subsequently Assistant Managing Editor. He also edited *The Railway Year Book*, to which readers were often referred in the *RM*'s 'The Why & The Wherefore' pages. His obituary in *RM* commented that 'his ability in placing a large number of detailed facts and figures in a clearly arranged and comprehensive manner is well illustrated by the many additions and improvements which he effected in what has become an acknowledged handy book of reference in all railway offices'.

His own *Why & Wherefore* book first appeared in 1911, and was followed by a second edition three years later. A number of other books by him were also published, and he had a wide acquaintance with many of the leading railway engineers of his day. He became one of the

John Francis Gairns
Editor 1910-1930

earliest members of the Railway Club, and the Institution of Railway Engineers, and was also a founder member of the Institute of Transport (now the Chartered Institute of Transport with its world-wide membership).

In December 1930 Gairns became the first of two Editors of *Railway Magazine* to die in office, and the 'Appreciation' by C. S. L. that followed his obituary in our January 1931 issue referred to him as 'one of the most active and painstaking workers on our staff, and indeed, from the field of specialised journalism as a whole . . . His almost life-long interest in the subject of railways had qualified him in the fullest sense for discharging the duties attached to his calling and the responsible position he occupied therein . . . He died as he had lived, "in harness" – honoured for his ability and thoroughness as a worker and mourned for his many good qualities as a friend.'

Gairns had been one of a quartet of writers who had taken over 'British Locomotive Practice & Performance' after Rous-Marten's death in 1908, and Cecil J. Allen who had in 1911 taken over the column himself, also began his February 1931 article in the series with a tribute to him. 'By the share which he took in the dissemination of well-informed and accurate publicity about the railways, in articles, books and lectures, he did much to help arouse the public interest in railway matters which the railways themselves have at length come to recognise as a publicity asset of no mean value.'

1930-1942

After the death of John Gairns, J. K. Taylor acted as Assistant Editor in charge of production, *Railway Magazine* by then being part of John Kay's Tothill Press. Then, in 1932, at the age of

41, William Arthur Willox (1891-1970) became Editor of *Railway Magazine* and also Chief Assistant Editor of *Railway Gazette,* being noted as a stickler for correct grammar and syntax. By this time, the *RG* had established itself as an important weekly magazine dealing with professional railway matters and, under Kay's ownership, a useful synergy developed between the two publications dealing with much the same material, but for very different markets.

Willox had been educated at the City of London School and the City & Guilds (Engineering) College in South Kensington. After spending two years as a pupil under his father, who was Engineer of the Metropolitan Railway, he joined the Army in World War I, and was commissioned into the Royal Engineers. In 1942 he joined up again, and served as a major at the War Office until he retired in 1949. During the Salonika campaign in World War I, he had recovered from malaria by means of a nature cure and after his retirement he opened a nature-cure resort in Worcestershire, being its director at the time of his death in 1970.

John Aiton Kay (1883-1949) was one of the most 'formidable' characters in railway publishing. After being educated at Mill Hill School, at the age of 15 he joined the publishing empire of George Newnes, some of whose profits had been used to back the construction of the Lynton & Barnstaple Railway. Kay's first job was to run the model-engineering section of the well-known boys' magazine *Captain*. From there he moved to become the Assistant Editor of the weekly paper *Transport,* founded in 1892. His starting salary was £3 10s 0d (£3.50) per week, paid weekly, but he was entitled to a commission of 10 per cent on the net value of any advertisements he obtained, any special copies he could sell, and any new subscribers he could take on. During his first two years in the job, his total commission came to £11 16s 10d (£11.85). This periodical was American-owned, and by 1904 had become *Transport & Railway Gazette,* 'a journal of transportation, engineering and railroad news, covering railways, docks, harbours, contracts, shipping and general engineering'. The following year the title, at least, was simplified – and anglicised to – *Railway Gazette.*

In 1910 Kay paid a visit to the United States of America, ostensibly on holiday. Before he left he had borrowed money from his various UK advertising contacts, and with this bought the magazine from its American owners. Having left as Assistant Editor, he returned as Managing Director & Secretary of his own company,

William Arthur Willox
Editor 1932-1942

John Aiton Kay
Editor 1942-1949

Transport (1910) Ltd – a remarkable transformation, especially at the age of 27. From this beginning he went on to extend his railway publishing empire, taking over *Railway Times* in 1914, which had itself absorbed the pioneering *Herepath's Railway Magazine,* dating back to 1835. In 1916, he purchased *Railway Magazine* (from Sir Joseph Lawrence), and at roughly two-yearly intervals after, *Railway News,* and *Railway & Travel Monthly.* In 1920 the last-named was retitled *Transport & Travel Monthly,* before being merged with *Railway Magazine* three years later.

Kay's publishing business was combined into the Tothill Press in 1921, based at 33 Tothill Street, Westminster, and subsequently became the Railway Publishing Company. Later it was to find itself strategically situated between the Houses of Parliament and the Broadway headquarters of London Transport. As well as his railway titles, many other monthly technical journals were produced, covering such diverse subjects as *The Crown Colonist, Colliery Engineering, The Industrial Chemist, Coke & Gas,* and *Water Power.*

1942-1949

When Willox was called up in 1942, Kay became Editor of *Railway Magazine,* having taken great personal interest in it since purchasing a copy of the first issue 45 years earlier. One of his particular concerns was to ensure a high standard of illustration, which he managed in spite of the rigours of World War II. From May 1942, *Railway Magazine* had only appeared every other month because of paper shortages, and, shortly before becoming, in July 1949, at the age of 67, the second (and hopefully last!) Editor to die in office, Kay had agreed the

plans to resume monthly production from the beginning of 1950.

1949-1970

For 21 years, between 1949 and 1970, *Railway Magazine* did not have an 'Editor' as such, being produced by specialist journalists under the overall command of an Editor-in-Chief who, by all accounts, had no day-to-day hand in the preparation of the magazine whatsoever.

On the sudden death of John Kay, Basil W. Clifton Cooke, the Editor of *Railway Gazette,* became Editor-in-Chief of both it and *Railway Magazine.* Under him, also as Managing Editor of both publications, was Henry M. Dannatt, who had been one of Oliver Bulleid's 'bright young men' on the Southern Railway before joining the staff of the North British Locomotive Company. The Deputy Editor, who was effectively in charge of *Railway Magazine,* was Hugh Aymer Vallance, author of several papers to the Railway Club, whose book *The Highland Railway* had appeared in 1938. In 1963, Vallance retired because of ill-health, and was succeeded as Deputy Editor by John H. Court, another former member of staff of the North British Locomotive Company. His tenure in editorial charge of *Railway Magazine* lasted until November 1966, when there was a monumental row about his failure to return transparencies, photographs and articles to contributors, which caused one of them to serve Basil Cooke with a writ.

Meanwhile, in 1964, Tothill Press had been taken over by Odhams, which, in turn, became part of the International Publishing Corporation empire (IPC), which still owns the *Railway Magazine* title. At the end of that year they moved offices to the former *Picture Post* building, Hulton House in Fleet Street.

After Court had departed, the job of running *Railway Magazine* was taken over by John Slater and Gordon Flower, as joint Assistant Editors. Neither of their names appeared on the masthead, but those of Basil Cooke and Henry Dannatt did, although they primarily concerned themselves with the weekly issues of *Railway Gazette*, rather than the monthly publication for enthusiasts. In 1970 the *Gazette* ceased to be sold through the trade, and became a 'controlled-circulation' publication. Henry Dannatt was not in favour of the change, and left the company.

1970-1989
Because of the very different nature of the two associated railway titles, it was decided to split the editorial teams, and John Slater became Editor of *Railway Magazine* in 1970 with Gordon Flower as Assistant Editor. The previous long editorial hierarchy was then simplified, with Basil Cooke's name appearing under theirs on the masthead as 'Publishing Director'. He retired in 1972, and during the subsequent 25 years, the magazine has come under the control of several publishing directors, including Gavin Doyle, Dennis Holman, Martin Morgan, David Eckles, John Crookshank, Simon Thompson and the current publisher is Stephen Curtis.

John Ninis Slater was born in 1928 at Blackdown, Surrey, and educated at Fernden School, Haslemere and Wellington College, Crowthorne. In 1946 he began a five-year special engineering apprenticeship with the firm of Mather & Platt in Manchester, where he also studied at the colleges in nearby Newton Heath and Salford. In 1953 he was moved to the firm's London office, and subsequently saw better career opportunities at *Railway Gazette*, which he joined as Editorial Assistant in 1964.

During this time a number of developments had taken place with *Railway Magazine* itself. From the earliest days, colour frontispieces had appeared in certain issues but, with the switch to the larger format in November 1963, a 6¼in x 7¼in colour photograph was used on the cover each month. Until the mid-1950s, *Railway Magazine's* cover design had remained virtually unchanged for decades. A single monochrome illustration, in a circular or rectangular box, appeared in the bottom half, with the issue date, number and volume in scrolls below it, inside a coloured background. Readers unable to identify the location or subject of the illustration had to await the next issue, when it was repeated, with a caption, inside. During Court's time as Deputy Editor the cover was tidied up, the scrolls, etc.

removed, and a larger, rectangular illustration provided, but still in monochrome.

Another change has taken place in the way the news sections and feature articles appear in the magazine. In the early issues, the 'Illustrated Interview' began on the first page, facing the frontispiece if there was one. Other articles followed, with the news items in the form of 'What the Railways are Doing' and 'Pertinent Paragraphs' coming at the back. By the end of the 1940s the first page or two were occupied with an editorial. Later still this was supplemented with a page of 'Topics', but subsequently this was dropped, and the editorial came down to a single item on the first page with the masthead, an illustration and the list of contents. Then in July 1987 the cover carried a banner 'WITH ALL THE NEWS UP FRONT', and effectively, after 90 years, the order of items in the magazine had been completely reversed. Nowadays the editorial team very largely fill the pages in reverse order, the latest 'Headline News' coming on the first pages after the list of contents, which now includes illustrations as 'tasters'.

A large organisation like IPC has to optimise the use of its premises, and, during Slater's editorship, *Railway Magazine* changed offices on three numerous occasions. In May 1969 they moved from Fleet Street to Greville Street near Hatton Garden, and then to Hatfield House, Stamford Street, SE1, in October the same year. A move across the road saw them in Dorset House until November 1980, when they moved out to Quadrant House, an impressive tower block in Sutton. Throughout all this wandering they had kept close to their colleagues in the associated *Railway Gazette International*, whose title had acquired its 'international' aspect in 1971.

In 1986, however, the two magazines were allocated to separate business groups within IPC. *Railway Gazette International* became part of

John Ninis Slater
Editor 1970-1989

Reed Business Publishing, and remained at Sutton, where, at the time of writing they are still based. *Railway Magazine* joined a group known as Prospect Magazines, and moved to Prospect House, Ewell Road, Cheam. This was quite close to the railway station, but one had to allow a disproportionate amount of time to catch a train. There was only a ticket barrier on one of the platforms, which could necessitate two journeys under the four-track formation through the subway, where the passageway was frustratingly divided longitudinally in two by wire-netting!

1989-1994
In 1989 John Slater took early retirement, but continues on a part-time basis as Editorial Consultant. He was succeeded by Peter Kelly, who came from East Midlands Allied Press, nowadays known as Emap. Born in 1944 at Warrington, he had attended Boteler Grammar School before spending four years with the *Newton & Golborne News* at Earlestown. He then moved to the Iliffe Press's weekly publication *Motor Cycling*, as test rider and reporter. After working in the head office of the *Warrington Guardian* series, and the *Northern Echo* at Darlington, he had three years as Editor of *Motor Cycle*. Following several further moves, he joined Emap to edit yet another motor-cycling publication, but in 1980 became Editor of *Steam Railway* and also produced a *Rocket 150* special that same year. He then launched *Rail Enthusiast* for Emap, subsequently becoming Managing Editor of that and *Steam Railway*, before switching from railways to edit *Yours*, a newspaper for senior citizens during which time he produced the pilot issue of *Old Glory*.

Four years after increasing in size to 8¼in x 10⅞in in January 1982, the format of *Railway Magazine* went up to full A4 size, with a colour illustration occupying the whole cover. Superimposed either on the top of the actual picture, or on a band of colour, is the magazine's masthead, which underwent a design change in January 1992.

The impact of the cover has become particularly important, as a lot of readers now buy on impulse, rather than placing a regular order, so the appearance of each issue can materially affect sales. Up to 1982, covers had remained relatively 'unfussy', but since then it has become necessary for 'cover lines' or 'tasters' to be included as 'come-ons' for the prospective purchaser, drawing attention to what is inside. A 'flash' may also be used to alert a casual reader to some special feature. Newsagents are frequently

Peter Kelly
Editor 1989-1994

short of shelf space, and consequently display publications with only the left-hand half of the cover showing. Cover lines and flashes must, wherever possible, be on that side, or there is a real risk of them being obscured by the next magazine, which could be a railway one from a rival publisher.

At the end of the 1980s it was competitively important to widen the news coverage of *Railway Magazine*, and Kelly recruited Chris Milner from industry to follow Gordon Flower, who retired as Assistant Editor in 1990. Milner was born at Loughborough in 1952, and lived for many years close to the Great Central line, where he was able to watch the final days of main-line steam. He spent just over twenty years in industry as an operations analyst, during which he had submitted photographs and articles to the railway press, covering modern traction as well as steam. He joined our magazine initially as a freelance, before becoming Assistant Editor.

At the same time, Colin J. Marsden, as Consultant Editor (Modern Traction), to give him his current title, started to look after the details of the present-day scene for *Railway Magazine*. Marsden was born in 1957 at Kingston upon Thames, and worked for 16 years on the motive-power side of the Southern Region, based at Waterloo. From secondman he graduated to driver, and then became an instructor, before leaving the railway and moving to Dawlish in 1988. He has written more than 50 books on modern traction and is also well-known as a photographer, undertaking assignments for the railways and the railway industry.

Both these members of the editorial team have built up a considerable network of contacts who provide news stories and illustrations for their respective fields, Milner being particularly involved in steam matters and preserved railways.

The writer of this centenary book text, whose first *Railway Magazine* article appeared in June 1952, retired from the National Railway Museum in 1987. This gave him time to contribute additional articles, over and above his regular 'Practice & Performance' series, and he became Chief Correspondent in 1990, remaining a freelance. The construction work for the Channel Tunnel prompted a supplement in the autumn of 1989, followed by his monthly series 'Channel Tunnel Update', which appeared regularly until the formal inauguration by Her Majesty The Queen and President Mitterand in 1994.

In 1991, the magazine's offices moved back into London after it had returned administratively to the IPC fold. The staff were initially based in No. 2 Hatfields, just across the road from King's Reach Tower, through the wall from Hatfield House where they had been over 20 years earlier. Subsequently they moved into King's Reach Tower itself, where they have changed floors several times since.

1994-

Peter Kelly returned to Emap in September 1994, and was succeeded as Editor of *Railway Magazine* by Nicholas Hugh Pigott. Nick was born a few hundred yards from the East Coast Main Line at Barnby Moor, Nottinghamshire, in 1951 and spent most of his childhood in a house overlooking the same line at Grantham, where he developed an abiding passion for Gresley's A3 Pacifics.

He was educated at Bromsgrove School, where he was fortunate to experience the end of regular steam working on the Lickey Incline. After leaving

Nicholas Hugh Pigott
Editor 1994-

school, he trained as a journalist on a number of Lincolnshire weekly newspapers before moving to the *Nottingham Evening Post* and *Birmingham Post*. At the age of 23, he achieved his ambition of reaching Fleet Street when he was appointed to the position of news sub-editor on the *Daily Express*, a paper he stayed with for twelve years. During that time, he undertook a solo round-the-world tour, his report and photographs being subsequently published as a two-page colour feature in the *Express*. He also became a qualified steam locomotive fireman on the standard gauge North Norfolk Railway.

His next staff appointments were with Emap, editing *Steam Railway* for four years as well as being Editor-in-Chief of *Steam World* before leaving to set up his own editorial business. It was through this company that he came to be associated professionally with *Railway Magazine* – a journal he had subscribed to for more than 30 years and to which he had first submitted material in 1965.

For a year before his appointment as only the seventh man to formally carry the title of Editor, he was a freelance feature writer and columnist for *Railway Magazine* and in 1994 launched and edited *Traction*, a new national railway periodical specialising in diesel and electric locomotives past and present.

SERIES COMPILERS AND COLUMNISTS

Railway Magazine is also famed for its series and specialist columns. It can boast the longest-running railway series in the world. This began as 'British Locomotive Practice & Performance', and the first of the articles by Charles Rous-Marten (1844-1908) with that title appeared in the September 1901 issue.

Rous-Marten had emigrated to New Zealand with his family at the age of 15, having already started compiling notes on the running of express trains. He became a journalist, but in 1887 was asked by his government to visit Britain and make a study of our railways, in the course of which he travelled some 40,000 miles. The official report created considerable interest world-wide and he was asked to make similar studies into the railways of five other countries.

He returned to England in 1893, in time to take part in recording details of the 1895 round of 'Races to the North'. On one occasion he jumped out of a train as it was running into the platform at Aberdeen and, complete with top hat and flying coat-tails, was assisted by the guard into an up train for Edinburgh which had just got just got the right-away. With the door safely closed, the guard turned to Rous-Marten and remarked, 'Ye'll no' be makin' a long stay in Aberdeen the morn!'. In 1904 he recorded *City of Truro's* hectic dash down Wellington Bank, as described elsewhere.

On Rous-Marten's death in April 1908, the 'Practice & Performance' series was taken over by R. E. Charlewood (1879-1950) for twelve months from that June. As a young man, Charlewood (the middle 'e' was pronounced) had lived at Morecambe Bay, adjacent to the London & North Western Railway's Lancaster & Carlisle section, over which he had travelled for some 28,000 miles by 1904. After reading law at Oxford, he joined the family law firm in Manchester, but was afterwards offered a job in the Midland Railway's Trains Office at Derby, where he worked until his early retirement in 1934. In 1935, travelling on a Frankfurt–Saarbrücken train, he was arrested by the German police after sketching a station layout. He was held in custody for nearly two months, most of the time in Berlin Moabit prison, and released following the intervention of Sir Josiah Stamp, the LMS President, and Dr Julius Dorpmuller, the German Minister of Transport. He later wrote privately a detailed account of his experiences, which provides an interesting insight into that country's prison regimes in the 1930s as well as his own feelings.

From June 1909 until the beginning of 1911 the series was shared by Rev. W. J. Scott, J. F. Gairns and Cecil J. Allen. The last named then took over single-handed until the end of 1958, contributing no less than 535 articles during the half-century. Allen (1886-1973) joined the Great Eastern Railway in 1903, and his first article for *Railway Magazine* was a three-part one on that railway's expresses, which appeared in 1906. He also wrote under pen-names such as 'Mercury' and 'Voyageur'.

There has been just one break in the whole series, in September 1930. Allen had prepared the article, seen the proofs into page, and then went on holiday. Gairns, the Editor, was very friendly with Gresley, and considered the article was too critical of the LNER Pacifics, so 'spiked' it. In the magazine that month a note referred to the article being held over 'due to unavoidable circumstances', but it was never published, and is no longer on file.

Allen gave up the series at somewhat short notice soon after a dinner had been held in his honour, but continued to write on performance matters for the Ian Allan magazine *Trains*

Cecil J. Allen

Illustrated, which his son, Geoffrey Freeman Allen, then edited. Oswald Stevens Nock (1905-1994), a senior signal engineer at Westinghouse, and the most prolific railway author in the country, was quickly recruited to take his place. Over the next 22 years he contributed 264 articles, dropping the word 'British' from the title in the process, to enable overseas subjects to be included.

In the spring of 1980, John Slater met the writer on the platform at Keighley station before a special run by the restored *City of Wells*, and said that Nock wished to give up the series. The writer was asked to take over from the beginning of 1981 and, by the end of 1995, had contributed 180 articles in the series. The word 'Locomotive' was replaced by 'Railway' in 1992, because so many trains now consist of multiple units, rather than being locomotive-hauled, and more recently still, 'Railway' has been dropped, conforming with the present-day trend to eliminate unnecessary words!

'Practice & Performance' was not, however, the first column with which *Railway Magazine* was to be associated. That was 'The Why & The Wherefore', which appeared in November 1899 in response to requests for an 'information' page. There were strict rules: 'queries relating to the names, numbers, dates, dimensions &c of locomotives will in no case be answered (such information being of little general interest)'. Things have changed considerably since then, and lists of the latest renumberings now appear frequently in our 'News' and 'Traction Update' columns. Another early rule was that no answers would be given that could be found in the Tothill

publication *The Railway Year Book*, the implication being that *RM* readers should buy that as well.

After various breaks, 'The Why & The Wherefore' still appears, under the main title 'Answers', being looked after by John Slater. Fewer subjects are now dealt with each month, but at rather greater length. In the early days it was not unknown for the answer to be a simple 'Yes', nor can one any longer hear the swish of the head-master's cane as was all too obvious in some of the early replies!

In the February 1939 issue, George Sekon showed he was not averse to chiding his correspondents in public either, albeit quite some years after he had ceased to be Editor. Describing one of his very first contributors, he wrote: "The Rev. W. J. Scott was an advanced Anglo-Catholic; he prided himself on being a literary stylist – the opening of his contribution to the first number shows this. His handwriting was atrocious – he employed no typist – and he was always at a loss for illustrations. In these dilemmas he frequently fell back on plans and maps prepared by himself. Of these he was very proud; when they were more crude than usual and had to be re-drawn, he showed resentment. Unfortunately, he was that nightmare of editors – never ready with his 'copy' at the agreed date!"

Book reviews – 'Railway Literature' – appeared at quite an early stage, and form a useful guide for readers. In recent years, they have been joined in the 'Railfare' section by reviews of videos, and the pages have been enlivened by colour reproductions of their respective covers. Another important part of the magazine has been 'Coming Events', which covers any happening of

Oswald Stevens Nock

Peter W. B. Semmens

railway interest, ranging from a talk to special trains. It was introduced in May 1964 when steam on BR was in its final phase. Many tours were then being organised, and the number of societies holding meetings had increased considerably. In more recent days when hard-copy was still being sent to the typesetters, the material for a month's entries could occupy more than 30 A4 sheets. The publication of 'Letters to the Editor' began in 1954, and, after appearing as 'Mail Bag', is now 'Readers' Forum', with the Editor selecting a 'Letter of the Month'.

'What the Railways are Doing' appeared in our first issue, and a section with this title appeared for a long time. In recent years the demand for up-to-date information about the latest happenings on the country's railways has seen a rapid expansion of the space required for the information, and a high proportion of the magazine is now devoted to 'News'. A section on 'Locomotive Notes', or latterly 'Traffic & Traction', used to be included in the news at the end of the magazine, and a couple of decades ago would have occupied a few pages of text, relieved by one or two illustrations. Now we have numerous pages, besprinkled with colour photographs, devoted to 'Traction & Rolling Stock' and 'Steam News', 'Network News' and 'Operations News', in addition to a section on 'Preserved Traction News'.

Another long-running series was Ernest Leopold Ahrons' 'Locomotive & Train Working in the Latter Part of the Nineteenth Century', which appeared in serial form between 1915 and 1926. Ahrons was born in Bradford in 1866, and at 19 became an engineering pupil at Swindon under William Dean, following this with two years in the drawing office there. After that he held a number of engineering appointments at home and abroad, before devoting himself entirely to writing from the age of 53. His comprehensive and authoritative study, *The British Steam Locomotive from 1825 to 1925*, was written for *The Engineer* to mark the 1925 Stockton & Darlington Centenary. Subsequently published in book form, it was reprinted as recently as 1987.

Ahrons had much first-hand information about railway operating in the late 1800s, and was able to describe what he had observed very clearly. He also enlivened his accounts with humour, as the start of his article on the Lancashire & Yorkshire Railway shows:

'There is no railway in Great Britain that has undergone such radical and complete changes as the Lancashire and Yorkshire. In the middle of the 'seventies it was probably the most degenerate railway in the kingdom, to which even the South Eastern or the London, Chatham and Dover could have run only a bad second. And this was in spite of the fact that the Lancashire and Yorkshire was essentially a commercial railway used almost entirely by business men and the working classes. No annual Christmas pantomime in either of the two counties of the roses was complete without a constant running commentary on the misdoings of this railway, and a topical song devoted almost entirely to it. One such Yorkshire chorus had it that–

"He went to Bradford for to dine
By the Lancashire and Yorkshire line
He waited three weeks at bleak Low Moor,
And when he complained the porter swore
That he ought to have started a month before,"
etc., etc.

It was wretched doggerel, but it went down exceedingly well with the public, as it was a popular theme, upon which both counties of the roses were absolutely unanimous, albeit they disagreed over many other questions, from former English Kings down to modern county cricket.

A feature of the Lancashire and Yorkshire landscape of this period was the extremely high percentage of red-headed individuals amongst the traffic staff. Just as every London and South Western employee to-day (1917) has to wear a red tie, so it would appear that many of the Lancashire and Yorkshire functionaries of those days had to be provided with red hair. Their heads were not used for the purpose of signalling trains to stop, as far as I am aware, for the trouble then was to get trains to start, and they would pull-up either on the very slightest provocation, or on none at all.'

A later series of articles from the *Railway Magazine* by David L. Smith was also reprinted in book form, this time by Ian Allan in the 1960s. On the suggestion of Cecil J. Allen, David Smith had written the first of his humorous articles, 'G. & S. W. Nights' Entertainments', in 1939. Years later, the writer still bursts into laughter when re-reading them. One of the stories concerned the Portpatrick & Wigtonshire route, which was not equipped with single-line tablets until the late 'eighties:

'I had an aged relative, one Will McGill, who fired on the 'Port Road Paddy' (Irish boat train) from Stranraer to Carlisle the first night the tablets were installed. They came to Kirkcowan. The signalman was standing on the edge of the platform to deliver the tablet, his wife had hold of his arm, his son held the wife's arm and with the other embraced the paling – 'For fear,' as McGill said, 'that he would be *sookit* in!'

Finally, no account of *Railway Magazine* would be complete without mention of Brenda Brownjohn, the Editor's Secretary. Her work entails handling a vast volume of correspondence, articles and photographs as well as keying-in hundreds of submitted features and letters, and her patient and meticulous care in checking editorial copy and proofs prevents many errors from making an appearance in the finished product.

A CENTURY OF MAJOR RAILWAY EVENTS SEEN THROUGH THE COLUMNS OF *RAILWAY MAGAZINE*

MANCHESTER, SHEFFIELD & LINCOLNSHIRE RAILWAY BECOMES THE GREAT CENTRAL (1897)

A month after the first issue of *Railway Magazine* appeared, the Manchester, Sheffield & Lincolnshire Railway (MSL), formed in 1846, altered its name to Great Central. In the days when railways had nicknames based on their initials, it was said the change was from Money Sunk & Lost, (or Mucky, Slow & Lazy) to Gone Completely!

The MSL, as its name implied, was a cross-country line, stretching from Southport to Grimsby, and the reason for the name change was its London Extension. This ran from Beighton, near Sheffield, to Quainton Road and Ashenden, from where its small Marylebone enclave was reached over the tracks of the Great Western and Metropolitan Railways.

Our first issue included an article by B. Fletcher-Robinson, 'The New 'Great Central' Railway Extension to London', with a map of the line and several illustrations of the construction work in progress. Describing the reasons for the extension, he commented that the MSL 'had no line to London, for which they had just cause for grumbling. But they found themselves in the exasperating position of acting as jackals to their more fortunate rivals already possessing London termini'.

Under the 'Great Central' heading in 'What the Railways are Doing' for February 1899, it is stated that 'The London extension is rapidly approaching completion, if the contractors are to be relied upon, and "wind, weather (of importance in railway construction) and other circumstances permitting", the formal opening will take place shortly'. Two months later, after the formal opening had taken place on 9th March, we reported that 'Only four passengers travelled by the first train that left Marylebone Railway Station – the first passenger train on the new line. Having regard to the fact that the hour was 5.15 in the morning, and that no effort was made by the Company to acquaint the public with the service, the small number was not surprising.' Remarkably similar comments on both counts were to be

The words on the lips of every 'railwayac' in 1897 concerned the construction of what was to become Britain's last full-length main line for at least another 100 years – the Great Central Railway's London Extension. The GCR title was created when the Manchester, Sheffield & Lincolnshire Railway changed its name just a month after the launch of the RM. It is difficult to conceive from a late-1990s standpoint that a line whose closure is now considered 'ancient history' by many readers under the age of 40 had yet to be opened when this magazine was started. This scene shows construction work c1897.

made 95 years later about the Channel Tunnel and its operations!

Most of the Great Central's London Extension was closed in the post-Beeching era.

CITY OF TRURO'S SPEED RECORD (1904)

In the 1900s, the Great Western and London & South Western railways were rivalling each other to take passengers and mail to London after they had arrived in Plymouth off trans-Atlantic liners.

The GWR was improving its West of England services, which then ran via Bristol, and took every opportunity to set new records. On 9th May 1904 Charles Rous-Marten, the founding author of our 'Practice & Performance' series, was travelling on a five-van 'Ocean Mail Special' hauled by the outside-framed 4-4-0 *City of Truro*. They did not dawdle as far as Exeter, but it was between there and Taunton that the real fireworks occurred. After leaving Whiteball Tunnel they made 'a hurricane descent [of Wellington Bank], . . ., which was nearly spoiled, however, by a check near the station through some foolish platelayers calmly staying on the 'four-foot' when the

'lightning special' was close on them'. Even so, he claimed a maximum of 102.3mph, which so frightened the GWR 'Powers that Be' that the details were hushed up until 1922, by which time Rous-Marten was dead.

In 1934 Cecil J. Allen devoted considerable space to the run in several of his 'Practice & Performance' articles, but the discussions were not based on the original figures. In 1954, to mark the fiftieth anniversary of the exploit, O. S. Nock carried out an exhaustive analysis of the data, and the writer also discussed the matter in his April 1983 'Practice & Performance' article. While an accuracy to one place of decimals cannot be claimed for stop-watch recordings, there are strong indications that the train reached 100mph before the brakes went on. One other query remains: was there any real likelihood of a brake application at 100mph making any difference to the lives of the track-gang, or did Driver Clements decide he was already going faster than he thought safe?

A colour illustration of *City of Truro* appears on page 40.

'CORNISH RIVIERA' INTRODUCED (1904)

In 1904, the Great Western introduced a new express from Paddington to Penzance, running via Bristol. As the July issue of *RM* put it, 'For many months past it has been an open secret that the Great Western Railway intended to run from Paddington to Plymouth (and *vice versa*) without an intermediate stop. This world's record for a long distance run is now possible because Mr Inglis [the company's General Manager] has had put down at Exminster "Ramsbottom" pick-up water troughs. The marvellous results attained by the "mail specials" which were chronicled in last month's issue of the RAILWAY MAGAZINE, whetted the appetites of *railwayacs* for some startling timings. The time table shows that they will not be disappointed, . . .'

The *RM* offered a three-guinea (£3.15) prize to name the train – 'An Interesting and Easy Competition'. There were nearly 2,000 entries, but a third were ineligible because they were sent directly to the GWR. The prize was awarded jointly to two readers who had suggested 'The Riviera Express', but the train itself was named 'The Cornish Riviera' in 1905 because of the tourist potential.

As the 'Cornish Riviera Express' or 'Cornish Riviera Limited' – it has operated ever since the 1906 switch to the Westbury route, featuring frequently in the *RM*'s news and photographic pages. After the World War I slowings had ended, Cecil J. Allen made a round trip on it to Penzance, at the time when slip coaches were dropped at Westbury, Taunton and Exeter in the down direction. His account appeared in the December 1921 'Practice & Performance', with *Lode Star*, now on display at the NRM, recovering 15 minutes lost from checks *en route*. More recently, an HST with its 3-hour journey to Plymouth inclusive of a stop at Exeter, featured in one of the writer's 'Practice & Performance' articles.

THE GREAT BEAR (1908)

Included with the *RM*'s October 1908 issue was: 'A colour plate of the Great Western Railway's *Pacific* type, locomotive No. 111, "The Great Bear", designed by Mr G. J. Churchward, Locomotive Superintendent'.

This first tender 4-6-2 locomotive in the UK, completed at Swindon in February that year, looked very impressive in its lined livery with a large-diameter, copper-capped chimney, but its performance did not match its appearance. Route availability was limited, and the rear axleboxes tended to overheat. When word got

Although the LNER, LMS and Southern Railways later became famed for their impressive fleets of Pacific locomotives, Britain's very first 4-6-2 tender engine was built, curiously, by a railway which later shunned the concept and was never to build another. The Great Western constructed No. 111 The Great Bear in 1908, but 16 years later rebuilt it as a conventional 'Castle' class 4-6-0.

around in 1922 that Gresley was designing a Pacific, someone at the GWR is reported to have said, 'I don't know why that young man at Doncaster is building one, when we could have sold him ours'. No. 111 was nominally rebuilt as a 'Castle', *Viscount Churchill*, in 1924 but, although confined to the Great Western route between London and Bristol in its original form, it had nevertheless managed to run over half a million miles during its 16 years as a Pacific.

WORLD WAR I (1914-1918)

Railway happenings at home and abroad were reported in far more detail in *Railway Magazine* during World War I (1914-1918) than during the 1939-1945 conflict. To a considerable extent this was due to the supplies of paper available. Although the quality undoubtedly deteriorated, the July–December volume in 1918 contained 426 pages, only 15 per cent less than the corresponding one four years earlier. During 1917 an appeal to send a friend in the forces a copy was being used as a page filler.

Our home railways were also not so badly affected directly by the First World War. The mobilisation of the Territorial Forces in August 1914 caused a brief dislocation of public services, our October 1914 issue having a feature, 'Railway "Business as Usual"'. There were no widespread cuts until the beginning of 1917, details of which were duly reported in our columns. October 1914 saw the start of a long 'Ambulance Trains on British Railways' series, and the first 'Pertinent Paragraph' that month was entitled 'British Railways "Nationalised"', referring to their take-over by the Railway Executive Committee.

Looking back, *Railway Magazine*'s coverage of the war was, to a considerable extent, similar to that of *Railway Gazette*'s in 1939-1945, and included a long series 'British Railway Service and the War'. In late 1914 there were also articles on the railways of our continental allies, as well as the enemies', not to mention military railway movements in the Empire. Censorship of military activities likely to be of use to the enemy was to come later!

Our first issue after the end of the war carried a paragraph on Sir John Aspinall's presidential address to the Institution of Civil Engineers. Exactly four years earlier, we had reported his experiences after he had been interned when war broke out, which caught him on holiday in Germany. Some details were given of a long journey in a goods van, before he and his companions were marched to a camp. It seems surprising that the Germans should have released him. They had acknowledged that his age would prevent him from serving in the forces, but his subsequent contribution to our railways' war effort was far greater than any individual soldier could have made.

QUINTINSHILL DISASTER (1915)

On 22nd May 1915, a double collision at Quintinshill sidings, just north of Gretna, on the Caledonian Railway, caused an estimated 227 fatalities, with 246 injured, the exact numbers never being determined. As our July issue commented, this was 'by far the worst railway accident the United Kingdom has known, while the death-roll, double that of the Armagh accident, which previously held the record, included many members of His Majesty's forces travelling in connection with their military duties'. At that time few details were available, although it was reported that the signalman primarily concerned had been arrested on a charge of culpable homicide.

In fact two signalmen were involved, who had unofficially switched their shift times, and, as part of the cover-up, proper records were not being made in the train register. The local train on which one of them had arrived from Carlisle was stopped, shunted on to the other track, and then forgotten. A southbound troop special was accepted, and collided violently with the local, its 15 coaches being reduced to a 67-yard pile of debris. Before anyone could react, a double-headed northbound express charged into the wreckage. Two coal trains in sidings alongside the main lines were also involved in the subsequent fire.

The inquiry into the accident was carried out by Lt-Col. Druitt, who placed the blame on the signalmen, who were given prison sentences for manslaughter. A summary of his report appeared in our November 1915 issue, which included recommendations for reducing the likelihood of fire after a major accident.

In 1994 it was announced that a memorial to those killed would be placed in a nearby tourist centre.

FIRST GNR PACIFIC (1922)

The appearance of Gresley's first Pacific in 1922 coincided with *Railway Magazine*'s twenty-fifth anniversary, and much of the commemorative issue in June that year was taken up with descriptions and photographs of No. 1470 *Great Northern*. Charles Lake remarked in his article that the locomotive was the first express-passenger machine to be built at Doncaster for eleven years, and four months were to elapse before the second of the class appeared.

These Class A1 locomotives looked imposing, but their performance was not initially outstanding, which was confirmed three years later by the GWR/LNER Locomotive Exchanges (see below). Gresley had not fitted long-travel valves, against the advice of his staff, which made the locomotives sluggish and increased their fuel consumption. When the valve-gear of No. 2555 *Centenary* was modified in 1927, the results were dramatic, with the coal usage coming down from 50 to less than 40lb/mile. Swindon's supremacy had gone for good!

Together with the higher-pressure A3s that followed, there were eventually 79 non-streamlined Gresley Pacifics, which were always popular with the travelling public and enthusiasts alike. Numerous notable runs were made by them and described by Cecil J. Allen in his 'Practice & Performance' series, including the 100mph record of No. 4472 *Flying Scotsman* in 1934, and the 108mph achieved by No. 2750 *Papyrus* a year later. The class also pioneered long-distance non-stop running, first to Newcastle and then to Edinburgh.

GROUPING (1922/23)

In 1921, Parliament, after considering the idea of nationalising the country's railways, passed the Railways Act, under which more than 100 separate companies were to be combined into four large 'Groups'. These were still private companies which, to a large extent, served separate segments of Great Britain. Opportunities for competition were considerably reduced, but, where these still existed, such as with the Anglo-Scottish services, bouts of intense rivalry were to break out again from time to time. To ensure that the railways did not exploit their near-monopolies for medium- and long-distance goods and passenger traffic, the Railway Rates Tribunal was created, and continued to exert its influence until well into the nationalisation era.

The existing railways came together in two different ways, the major ones being known as 'Constituent' companies and the others 'Subsidiary' ones. Contrary to popular belief, the amalgamations did not all take place on 1st January 1923. For example, the enlargement of the GWR occurred on four different dates between 1st January 1922 and 1st July 1923. By and large, the more profitable the companies were, the sooner they were brought into the fold.

Our January 1923 'Pertinent Paragraphs' section briefly described the new groupings, and the way in which shareholders had agreed the changes. Further details and statistics occupied the first 16 pages of the February issue, which began:

'As from January 1, 1923, nearly all the railways, which have for so long supplied the railway transportation needs of Great Britain, have come within the all-embracing scope of one or other of the four "great" companies ordained by the Railways Act of 1921. As a result, the entire railway situation is radically altered, many of the famous "frontier" stations have lost their importance altogether, or merely retain it in a very much reduced and almost incidental form . . .'

Few would have expected that, after 25 years of Grouping, and 46 of Nationalisation, not to mention the development of fierce road and air competition, some of the 'frontier station' rivalries would once more break out in the mid-1990s, to the detriment of passengers' convenience.

STOCKTON & DARLINGTON RAILWAY CENTENARY (1925)

The 'Railway Centenary' was celebrated in 1925, 100 years after *Locomotion* had trundled its way from Shildon to Stockton along the Stockton & Darlington Railway. Coming two years after the Grouping, the anniversary provided the LNER, the lineal descendant of that railway, with a splendid opportunity for publicity.

Although the anniversary date was 27th September, in our January 1925 issue the editor led off with the first of eleven special articles on 'The Romance of the Railway Centenary', which began:

'There must be very few of our readers, including those who have lived long enough to see their sons and daughters grow up to be men and women, to whom the existence of railways and the availability of railway transport for almost any desired journey, has not, from their earliest years, constituted a commonplace of life.'

The main events of the year took place at the beginning of July, when a major railway exhibition was staged at Darlington and an

Early tangible evidence of the Grouping . . . the letters L M & S R on the tender of ex-Lancashire & Yorkshire Railway Hughes 4-6-0 No. 1662 on 9th January 1923. The Grouping consolidated more than 100 railway companies into the 'Big Four' – comprising the London Midland & Scottish (LM&SR), London & North Eastern (L&NER), Southern (SR) and Great Western (GWR). The ampersands were later dropped from the tender and tank sides of LMS and LNER locomotives.

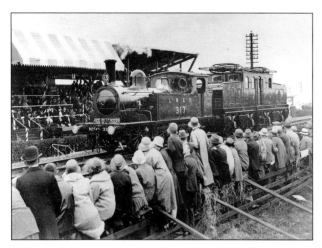

A major event of 1925 was the huge celebration to mark the centenary of the Stockton & Darlington Railway. Billed as the 'Railway Centenary', the event's highlight was a cavalcade of 53 locomotives and trains along part of the original S&D route in July of that year. The large amount of interest among the female contingent of the populace (attracted perhaps by the presence of the Duke and Duchess of York in the grandstand) is evident in this photograph of LNER Bo-Bo (later Class EB1) electric locomotive No. 9, built at Darlington in 1915 for the North Eastern Railway's Shildon-Newport electrification scheme. It is being towed past one of the grandstands at Goosepool by J71 0-6-0T No. 317. NRM

international congress held in London. They were preceded by a cavalcade of 53 locomotives and trains along part of the original S&D route, with the Duke and Duchess of York (later King George VI and Queen Elizabeth) watching from the grandstands at Goosepool, alongside what is today Teesside Airport. Reports about these events filled exactly half of our August issue, the Editor reporting that the celebrations:

'. . . were characterised by effective organisation at every stage, so that each item in the comprehensive programme arranged proceeded strictly according to plan and with never a suggestion of hitch or complication.'

The motive power and rolling stock in the cavalcade covered more than the full century, ranging from George Stephenson's rebuilt 1822 Hetton Colliery locomotive – in steam – to two brand-new LNER designs – the 2-8-0+0-8-2 Garratt and the three-cylinder, booster-fitted, Class P2 2-8-2 No. 2393. *Locomotion* itself brought up the rear, hauling a train of chaldron wagons, but was propelled by a petrol engine hidden in the tender. Considerable mirth resulted when members of the band playing in the wagons fell over when the train 'buffered up' alongside the grandstand.

The static display in Darlington Works included commemorative scrolls from the Chinese

delegates, and a massive 'shield' from the Italian railways. The latter was late arriving at Darlington, the wagon conveying it having got lost somewhere *en route*. With the press watching, it got jammed while being unloaded, and one of the Italians accompanying it gave vent to his annoyance with considerable eloquence for something like five minutes. Eventually the local interpreter explained to the reporters, 'The Senor is saying "Damn!"' Many of the historic exhibits subsequently found a home in the Railway Museum at York, which was opened to the public three years later and, in 1975, became part of the National Collection.

GWR/LNER LOCOMOTIVE EXCHANGES (1925)

At the British Empire Exhibition at Wembley in 1924, the GWR referred to its exhibit, *Caerphilly Castle*, as the 'most powerful express passenger locomotive in Great Britain' on the basis of its higher nominal tractive effort, when it appeared alongside the much larger LNER Pacific, *Flying Scotsman*. The following spring, exchange trials were arranged with the two classes, with a 'Castle' running between King's Cross and Doncaster, while a Gresley Pacific worked the 'Cornish Riviera' from Paddington to Plymouth.

For the public, the exchange became a major sporting event. In his summary of the running in the June issue of *Railway Magazine*, C. J. Allen, writing as 'Voyageur', commented that 'at some terminals and more important stops, policemen were needed to keep the enthusiastic observers under proper control'. Hundreds turned out at

The other highlight of 1925 was the great Locomotive Exchange, which saw the GWR and LNER pit their finest types against each other in a bid to see which railway had Britain's most powerful express passenger locomotive. GWR 'Castle' class 4-6-0 No. 4079 Pendennis Castle *makes a storming departure from King's Cross. NRM*

King's Cross to see *Pendennis Castle* tackle the bank to Finsbury Park. Many LNER staff were sceptical of it even clearing the 1-in-107 climb to Hornsey, but it walked away with the 16 bogies. The performance of *Caldicot Castle* on its own metals was also superior to that of the LNER's *Victor Wild*. On both routes the Pacifics burnt more coal and on the East Coast line, one of them failed with a hot box.

It had originally been intended that the detailed results of the exchanges would be kept confidential, but they were published in the June issue of *Great Western Railway Magazine*, and a summary sent to the press. The LNER's General Manager remonstrated with his opposite number about this, and received the answer that, as a member of the LNER staff – C. J. Allen – had been publicising them in broadcasts, the GWR was merely doing the same!

'CHELTENHAM FLYER' (1929-1939)

In 1923, the Great Western's afternoon train from Cheltenham was retimed at an average of 61.8mph over the Swindon-Paddington stretch. This was the fastest non-stop run in the country, and the train soon got the name 'Cheltenham Flyer'.

The first subsequent speed-up, in 1929, which lifted the average to 66.2mph and gave the train the fastest start-to-stop average in *the world*, was described in *RM* that September. After being briefly beaten by the Canadians in 1931, the GWR regained its supremacy five months later. On the first day of the new schedules it averaged 77.3mph from Swindon, which Cecil J. Allen described as a 'Record of Records' in the November *RM*, writing under his 'Mercury' pseudonym.

The next speed-up came in the autumn of 1932 when the 'Flyer' became the first train ever to be scheduled anywhere in the world at more than 70mph. By way of a preview, the GWR had laid on a *tour de force* for the benefit of three well-known recorders, C. J. Allen, Humphrey Baker and R. E. Charlewood. This involved no less than three service trains over the Swindon–Paddington stretch, starting with the 'Cheltenham Flyer'. The 'Flyer' ran at 90mph or faster for many miles of its journey, with a maximum of 92. At West Drayton, the locomotive was eased, but they were still doing 82 at Milepost 2, before stopping in Paddington 10¼ minutes early. The overall start-to-stop average worked out at 81.7mph. As Cecil J. Allen put it in a special article in the July *RM*, '. . . a world's record it is, in very truth, with no known superior or equal'.

MALLARD SETS WORLD RECORD FOR STEAM
(1938)

On Sunday 3rd July 1938 the LNER Pacific *Mallard* was nominally engaged on brake tests, but Gresley planned to use the run to beat the speed of 114mph set by the LMS the previous year. That had wrested the British record away from the LNER by just 2mph, and the East Coast authorities were anxious to regain it. As Cecil J. Allen put it in the first article in our August 1938 issue: 'When a record is broken, there is nothing like doing it thoroughly. And the LNER, in its brilliant speed achievement . . . carried its purpose into effect with such thoroughness as to leave the nearest British competitor some 11mph behind.'

Although at the time, a speed of only 125mph was claimed, a later analysis of the dynamometer-car roll showed a maximum of 126, which appeared on the post-war plaque fixed to the locomotive's streamlined casing. There was also some confusion over the record achieved by a German 4-6-4, and Driver Duddington's efforts with *Mallard* were not initially claimed as a world record until someone applied the correct kilometres/miles conversion factor!

World War II and its aftermath prevented any further record attempts, and in the 1950s, electric traction was to take over the speed supremacy from steam and diesel traction. *Mallard* was duly preserved and became one of the major attractions in the Museum of British Transport at Clapham, and subsequently at the National Railway Museum in York. With the help of Scarborough District Council and the museum's 'Friends', it was restored for a series of commemorative runs in the 1980s, but the highest speed permitted was less than half the maximum achieved fifty years before!

THE FIRST RAILTOUR (1938)

In June 1938, the LNER introduced some brand-new rolling-stock for its prestige train, the 'Flying Scotsman'. As part of the launch publicity, the Stirling 'Single' No. 1 in York Railway Museum was restored to working condition, and hauled the press party in GNR six-wheelers from King's Cross to Stevenage, where they transferred to the new train with the A4, *Sir Nigel Gresley*, at its head.

The interest created by this 'period' train prompted the LNER to run a public excursion from London to Cambridge in August, during which a speed of over 70mph was achieved. After this it went on public display at Alexandra Palace station – the one at the end of the now-closed branch line from today's station of the same name, which was then called Wood Green. On 11th September, the Railway Correspondence & Travel Society arranged a guaranteed excursion to Peterborough for 170 of its members, which became the first 'Rail Tour' run by a railway society in this country.

The outbreak of war prevented the idea catching on but, in the 1950s and 1960s, few major line-closures or withdrawals of notable steam classes were not marked by such a rail tour. One of the most spectacular to be run was the

Prelude to the first enthusiasts' railtour in September 1938. In June of that year, Stirling Single No. 1 is seen on a press special at Stevenage, alongside A4 No. 4498 Sir Nigel Gresley.

Stephenson Locomotive Society's 'Golden Jubilee' special in 1959, when Bill Hoole whisked *Sir Nigel Gresley* up to 112mph descending Stoke Bank.

WORLD WAR II (1939-45)

When the United Kingdom declared war on Germany in September 1939, Britain's railways were still the prime means of moving goods and people about the country. In the six years that followed, they were to be subjected to unprecedented attacks from the air, which was in marked contrast to the previous conflict. With the whole country in the front line, far more stringent control of the news was vital, and many railway happenings were said to have taken place 'somewhere in Britain'. Relatively little topical news could thus be printed about wartime traffic and happenings on our railway system, although 'Locomotive Notes' always appeared in our 'Notes and News' section.

Railway Magazine faced an even greater difficulty as paper was severely rationed during the war, particularly after the U-boat campaigns began in the Atlantic. Not only did the quality change for the worse, but the number of copies printed was severely limited. To overcome this, the magazine only appeared every other month from 1942 onwards, the total number of pages for that year being only 384, compared with 904 for 1939.

These restrictions continued during the post-war 'Austerity' period, and monthly publication did not resume until the 1950s. After VJ-Day, however, it was possible to recount a lot more of the railways' contribution to the war

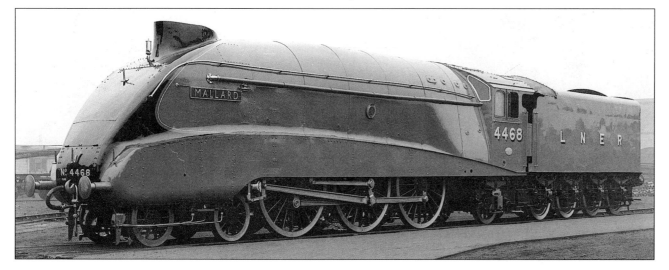

The all-conquering moment for steam traction came on 3rd July 1938 when LNER A4 No. 4468 Mallard *streaked down Stoke Bank, between Grantham and Peterborough, at a world-beating 126mph – a record which has never been beaten. The celebrity locomotive, restored to the external condition it was in at the time of the achievement, is now in the care of the National Railway Museum.*

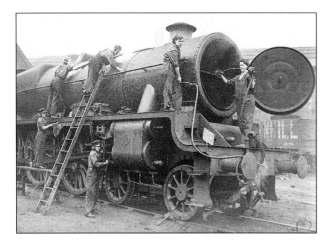

The Second World War, the end of which occurred roughly half way through the Railway Magazine's *100-year span, brought serious changes both in the way the magazine was produced (extremely thin issues produced just once every two months, combined with strict censorship), and in the way the railways operated. One big change was the extensive use of female labour in jobs hitherto considered male preserves, as exemplified by this photograph of women cleaners working on LMSR 'Jubilee' class 4-6-0 No. 5662* Kempenfelt *on 19th July 1941. Another change brought about by austerity was the imposition of unlined black on express passenger classes formerly associated with bright colour schemes. Streamlined 'Princess Coronation' Pacific No. 6245* City of London *was one so treated.*

British-built 'Austerity' locomotives were a common feature of the Second World War, but the American locomotive builders Alco, Lima and Baldwin were also engaged in a major construction programme. The first of many Class S160 2-8-0s built by these companies to the British loading gauge began arriving in Britain in November 1942, including Alco-built No. 1609, shown here being unloaded from a ship at Cardiff Docks. It is fittingly draped in a Union Jack for the occasion.

The terrible price of war . . . York station after a Nazi bomb blitz on the city in the early part of World War Two. The steel vestibule ends, still standing defiantly along the length of the platforms, are the only indication that two trains of wooden-bodied coaches once stood there. This picture was at first retained by the official censor, but was eventually released in July 1942.

somewhat brief outline, rather than to discuss fully, its manifold effects.'

Thus began an article by C. S. Denniss as long ago as our sixth issue (December 1897). He was then the General Manager of the Cambrian Railways, and in arguing against nationalisation, quoted the 'well-known' saying of George Stephenson, 'Let the country make the railroads, and the railroads will make the country'.

In both world wars, our railways were effectively nationalised, being run for the government by a committee of senior railway officers. Although nationalisation was seriously considered in the early 1920s, the 'Grouping' idea was chosen instead. In 1945 a Labour Government was elected, having included the railways amongst the numerous other organisations it proposed to nationalise, and the four Grouping companies ceased to exist at midnight on 31st December 1947.

Railway Magazine's paper ration was then still severely restricted, but our January/February issue for 1947 began with a two-page account of the Transport Nationalisation Bill, which covered canals, docks and road services, as well as the railways. A specially-painted frontispiece six months later showed one of the LNER B1s in 'Post Office Red', named *The New Era*. A two-page editorial in the first issue of 1948 included a broad outline of the six new BR Regions, while C. R. L. Coles contributed a longer article on 'The Grouping Era'. Within a few months new liveries were being tried out, and then came the Locomotive Exchanges which are described separately.

It was not, however, until 1950 that the first major reorganisation took place, when regional boundaries were primarily rearranged on a geographical basis rather than pre-Nationalisation ownership. This was 'with the object of simplifying supervision, reducing administrative costs and avoiding duplication'. The plan had a civil-service hall-mark, and produced many anomalies, some of which were subsequently readjusted, or disappeared with line-closures. It was only when BR implemented sector management in the 1980s that management was generally tied more sensibly to 'line of route'.

Many BR standards of different sorts were to appear in the years that followed, including locomotives, coaches, signals, track, timetables, signs, and even nomenclature ('Customers' instead of 'Passengers'). Many of these were to be revised more than once in the course of nearly half a century of Nationalisation.

effort, as well as giving details of the various 'New Works for Wartime Traffic', which were described in a two-part article by Charles E. Lee in the first half of 1946.

NATIONALISATION (1948)

'The nationalisation of railways is a subject of such enormous proportions, and its issues are so momentous to the entire community, that it is obviously impossible to more than indicate in

The year 1948 saw two events of enormous significance for the future of the railways – Nationalisation and the locomotive exchanges, the latter intended to determine the motive power policy of the newly-formed British Railways. It is difficult to illustrate Nationalisation itself, but this photograph neatly combines both events, depicting Stanier Pacific No. 46236 City of Bradford *in Sonning Cutting while working the 1.30pm from Paddington on 18th May that year. The freshly-applied lettering on the tender and the serif-style typeface on the smokebox numberplate are characteristic of the fledgling BR and were both short-lived.*

LOCOMOTIVE EXCHANGES (1948)

Within a few months of Nationalisation, British Railways announced plans for an extensive series of locomotive exchanges, involving express-passenger, mixed-traffic, and freight designs produced by the four Grouping companies. Lasting several months, they aroused considerable interest, as had been predicted by our editorial in the May/June issue that year.

'Although instituted as a means of obtaining information on which to base plans for future standardisation, an inevitable consequence of nationalisation, the announcement of the proposed exchange of locomotive power between the various Regions of British Railways was received with interest and speculation by locomotive enthusiasts everywhere.'

The express passenger designs involved were the GWR 'King', SR 'Merchant Navy', LMS 'Duchess' and 'Rebuilt Scot', and LNER A4, but gauge restrictions limited the 'Kings' to the Great Northern main line in addition to their own. For the mixed-traffic trials, the GWR 'Modified Hall', SR 'West Country', LMS 'Black Five' and LNER B1 class were involved, while the freight locomotives were 2-8-0s from the GWR, LMS, and LNER, with the addition of the WD 2-8-0 and 2-10-0 designs. The routes used extended from Plymouth to Inverness. Southern Region locomotives were

fitted with LMS tenders to enable them to pick up water from troughs on the 'foreign' routes.

A complicated system of operation was worked out, with visiting locomotives and their crews having a week to familiarise themselves with each route before a dynamometer car was attached behind them for three round-trip tests the following week. To eliminate one of the variables, a common grade of coal – from Yorkshire – was

used. The GWR considered their locomotives were designed for the Welsh variety, so additional tests were subsequently run using this fuel, which proved more to their locomotives' liking. Indeed the GWR 2-8-0 burning Welsh coal produced the highest efficiency recorded in any of the tests.

Unfortunately a lot of other conditions either were not or could not be standardised. On the LMS main line, the trains were at times very badly delayed, making the results meaningless. The A4s, *Mallard* included, suffered on several occasions from big-end overheating. On other routes some crews took liberties with sectional timings, running easily uphill, and making up time on the easier stretches, with consequent reduction in coal used.

As a result, the detailed report, published in 1949, contained only nine general conclusions. Summarising, each class was normally able to give a good account of itself over all routes, but average power requirements were low compared with the maximum needed. Wide fireboxes, large boilers, and high superheat all contributed to high efficiencies, but firing techniques had to be related to the coal used and design details such as the spacing of the firebars.

Further investigations were needed into the tendencies for some locomotives to slip, and to give irregular drawbar pulls. Mixed-traffic designs, with their smaller driving wheels, experienced no difficulty in reaching the speeds then required.

The old and the new: LMS-design diesel-electric No. 10001, hauling a fitted goods, overtakes ex-LNWR Class G2a 0-8-0 No. 49144 at the head of a rake of ex-works Underground stock near Bletchley in 1952.

Many features of the subsequent BR Standard locomotives were clearly influenced by these conclusions.

PRESERVATION OF TALYLLYN RAILWAY (1951)

Our 'Notes and News' section for January 1951 included the following item:

Future of the Talyllyn Railway

The future of the Talyllyn Railway has become uncertain, as Alderman Sir Henry Haydn Jones, who died in June last, was Manager, Secretary and virtual owner of the undertaking. A meeting of railway enthusiasts was held recently in Birmingham, to consider the position, and a committee was elected, with Mr W. G. Trinder as Chairman, and Mr P. Whitehouse as Hon. Secretary. The financial and material requirements of the railway are now being investigated, and the possibility of its continuing as a going concern are being considered. Readers interested in the preservation of this interesting narrow-gauge line should communicate with the committee. The Publicity Officer is Mr L. T. C Rolt . . .

Tom Rolt's enthusiasm got things moving, and a way was found to take over the line from Sir Haydn's widow. At that time, there was no precedent for a group of amateurs getting together to run a public railway, however

The preserved railway phenomenon, which was to play such an enormous part in the lives of enthusiasts following the end of BR steam in 1968, actually had its origin in the narrow gauge Talyllyn Railway, which was rescued as long ago as 1950 and first opened its doors as a leisure line in 1951. A rare pre-preservation view of this peaceful line at the height of World War II, seemingly a million miles from the ravages of the conflict, as Fletcher Jennings 0-4-0WT No. 2 Dolgoch ambles slowly through the sylvan glades in May 1941.

small and remote. Nevertheless our July issue that year had a photograph of the inaugural Society train at Towyn on Whitsun Monday, when the line was reopened as far as Rhydyronen. Both the Talyllyn locomotives were in a pretty bad way, but *Dolgoch's* 85-year-old boiler had passed the inspector's examination. This enabled the 'Old Lady' to be used until they were able to buy the two ex-Corris 0-4-2STs from the Western Region for £65 each, and restore the first of them to working order. The Railway Preservation Movement had begun.

John Slater, *Railway Magazine's* editorial consultant, is among the hundreds of volunteers who have since worked on the railway, editing the Society's magazine – *Talyllyn News* – as well as using his engineering skills in the line's workshop.

THE FIRST BR STANDARD LOCOMOTIVES (1951)

In late 1950 there was great interest in the announcement that British Railways would complete the initial batch of standard steam locomotives at Crewe the following year, and the first of them was formally named *Britannia* at Marylebone on 30th January. It was a mixed-traffic Pacific, and its clean styling was to be a common feature for all 999 locomotives that were built to the new designs. They ranged in size from Class 2MT 2-6-2 tanks to the massive Class 9F 2-10-0s. That summer, No. 70004 *William Shakespeare* was a popular exhibit at the Festival of Britain on London's South Bank, and was later used regularly on the 'Golden Arrow' – the 1950s equivalent of today's Eurostars.

All the standard designs had two outside cylinders, and numerous other features were adopted to simplify maintenance and operation, such as the use of grease lubrication. A lot of planning also went into the design of the footplate controls, to assist the job of the crews, who were becoming difficult to recruit in the 1950s. However, the use of a fixed cab floor extending over the front of the tender framing tended to give drivers a cold back.

Many of the 'Britannias' were allocated to the Eastern Region for services in East Anglia, where they revolutionised the Norwich services. In the August 1951 issue, Cecil J. Allen referred to a Liverpool Street–Norwich journey with No. 70001 *Lord Hurcomb* as '. . . a rousing affair'. A month earlier he had timed another of the class on the West Coast route which beat the pre-war schedule of the 'Coronation' between Blisworth and Willesden.

The year 1951 also saw the introduction of the first BR Standard locomotives. No. 70004 William Shakespeare is seen on its inaugural run on 11th October leaving Victoria with the 'Golden Arrow'.

THE HARROW & WEALDSTONE DISASTER (1952)

In the morning rush-hour on 8th October 1952, a disastrous double collision occurred in Harrow & Wealdstone station on the London Midland Region's main line out of Euston. The driver of an overnight sleeping-car train from Scotland failed to brake for the signals protecting the rear of a suburban train in the station, and collided with it violently. Seconds later the pile of wreckage was hit by a double-headed express in the opposite direction, the locomotives of which were flung across the down platform.

In terms of fatalities, the 112 killed made it the second-worst railway accident in Great Britain, but it was relatively easy for the MoT inspecting officer to determine the cause. Our December issue began with details of his initial conclusions, and illustrations showing the extent of the wreckage were included in our pictorial pages.

The locomotives involved included Pacific, No. 46202 *Princess Anne*, the former 'Turbomotive', which had been double-heading with 'Jubilee' No. 45637 *Windward Islands*. Both were written off.

The disaster focussed public attention on the use of 'Automatic Train Control', as it was then known, and work was pressed ahead with the final development and subsequent installation of the standard BR Advanced Warning System (AWS).

The carnage which resulted from the Harrow & Wealdstone triple smash on 8th October 1952 was so horrific that it lives for ever not only in the memories of those unfortunate to witness it, but also in those who have only ever seen photographs! With aerial pictures like this, that is hardly surprising. Taken from a specially-chartered aircraft, it shows hundreds of rescuers swarming like ants over the twisted wreckage strewn across seven tracks. 112 people perished in the disaster, the second worst death toll in British railway history.

THE 'DELTICS' (1955-1982)

In September 1951, the English Electric company started to design the most powerful diesel locomotive in the world, installing as prime movers a pair of Napier 'Deltic' engines, as used for naval gunboats. This 3,300hp prototype did not enter service until 1955, its appearance being marked in our December issue with an editorial reference to 'A Remarkable Prototype Diesel'. Elsewhere there was a description of the locomotive, but the monochrome illustration did not show off its remarkable powder-blue livery with aluminium side mouldings and yellow 'speed-whiskers' on its ends.

At the end of 1955, it went into passenger service on the West Coast route between Merseyside and London, and the occasional illustration appeared in *RM* from 1957 onwards, including one of it on test over the Settle & Carlisle in that year. In his 'Practice & Performance' article the following March, O. S. Nock referred to some of these tests when the diesel, with a load of 642 tons, breasted Ais Gill at 49mph, 3mph faster than the 'Jubilee' 4-6-0 No. 5660 *Rooke* had managed with less than half that weight during its outstanding 1937 trials.

With the East Coast electrification shelved, the Eastern, North Eastern and Scottish regions subsequently decided that something a lot better was needed than the 2,000hp English Type 4 (later Class 40) locomotives, which could be eclipsed on a good day by an A4 with a willing crew. Agreement was obtained to purchase a fleet of 22 production 'Deltics', and the prototype moved over to the Eastern Region in 1959, where Bill Hoole was able to demonstrate some of its capabilities before he retired in July that year.

It was not until 1961 that the first of the production locomotives entered passenger service but, from then until their withdrawal in January 1982, their achievements were rarely absent from our columns, particularly after 100mph running had been introduced in 1964. By popular demand, the writer's 'P&P' articles for January and April 1982 were both devoted to them, the latter finishing with a description of his impressions from the cab as the train passed through York on their final service run.

'As the driver opened the controller, and our twin Napier engines picked up from idling speed, we realised that there was actually a solid wall of spectators lining the whole length of Platform 8 (now No. 3), while others packed the footbridge and those sections of Platform 9 (now No. 5) not occupied by a stationary DMU. One could not envisage a more impressive tribute to the class of locomotives that set diesel traction on the right lines in this country and caught the imagination of thousands.'

THE BR MODERNISATION PLAN (1955)

The British Transport Commission's 1955 Modernisation Plan set in motion the most widespread *technical* changes ever made to this country's railway system, heralding the end of steam for normal traction purposes. After the Second World War the national economy had taken a long time to recover, with a high proportion of the country's resources being devoted to building houses and city centres lost during the Blitz, with little being done to catch up on six years of wartime wear and tear on our railways until 1955.

As the first editorial feature in our March 1955 issue reported:

'The outstanding feature of the recently-published plan . . . is the gradual replacement of steam

In diesel traction terms, there is little to beat a 'Deltic' in terms of power and enthusiast affection. The powder-blue liveried prototype attracted admiring glances wherever it went between 1955 and 1960 and was followed by a fleet of 22 production locomotives which formed the mainstay of East Coast motive power for the best part of two decades. In the class's first full year of service, No. D9018 Ballymoss passes Monktonhall Junction with the southbound 'Flying Scotsman'. Gavin Morrison

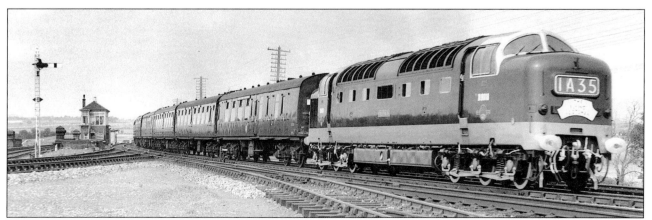

The Modernisation Plan of 1955 turned out to have some of the most far-reaching implications of any document in railway history. Among one of the many results of the wholesale drive to rid the railway of steam traction was the establishment of several purpose-built diesel maintenance depots. The Eastern Region was in the vanguard of such changes and this glass and steel structure at Finsbury Park, depicted on 21st April 1960, was typical of many erected during that era.

locomotives by diesel and electric traction. Of a total of £1,240million to be expended over 15 years, £345million is allocated for this purpose. Freight service improvements, including the fitting of continuous brakes to all wagons, over 250,000 new and larger wagons, and the re-siting and modernisation of many marshalling yards and goods terminals, are allocated £365million. Civil engineering works comprising improvements to the permanent way and signalling allowing of speeds up to 100mph on all principal trunk routes, are provided for at cost of £210million, and £285million will be spent on modernisation of passenger coaches, stations, and parcels depots. As a step in increasing the efficiency of the railways, the plan is certainly to be welcomed.'

More details were reported as time progressed, and included the electrification of the West Coast route to Liverpool and Manchester, the East Coast Main Line to Doncaster, Leeds, and possibly York, and Liverpool Street to Ipswich, including various branches.

By the end of the 15 years (1970) some 2,500 main-line diesels were expected to be at work, with steam having been eliminated west of Newton Abbot. DMUs were to be used for city-to-city express services, secondary and cross-country routes, and branch lines. At the end of the plan, a total of 4,600 such vehicles would be needed, while extensions to the Southern's third-rail network would require some 3,600 multiple-unit vehicles.

The replacement of steam-hauled trains on branch lines by DMUs was popular with the travelling public, and they were much more economical to operate. With the aid of the railway industry, large numbers of them were soon in service, but for a variety of reasons the other changes were delayed. As a result, the Plan had to be reappraised in 1959 and this hastened the demise of steam. At the beginning of 1955 BR had possessed 18,420 steam locomotives, but four years later there were still 16,959 on the books. Following the review, the diesel take-over accelerated. In 1959 the steam stock dropped by more than 2,500, and no less than 751 new diesel locomotives entered service in 1960.

WESTERN REGION DIESEL-HYDRAULICS
(1958-1977)

When BR's dieselisation was planned in the late 1950s, a 'Pilot Scheme' was initiated, with various designs being ordered and tested before full-scale production began. Unlike the other regions, which were promised electrification, the Western faced the fact that it would get none, even in the long-term, and was not enamoured of the heavy diesel-electric designs then available. It looked at the new West German diesel-hydraulic locomotives, and successfully argued that their markedly-better power:weight ratio would be beneficial for its routes. The absence of an electric transmission would also avoid the need to recruit electricians.

Slimming down the Berne-gauge German designs took a long time, and the first diesel-hydraulics to enter service were the five North British 'heavyweights' with their A1A-A1A wheel arrangement. When No. D600 *Active* was delivered in 1958, it was the first 2,000hp diesel built under the Modernisation Plan, and the class soon found itself on the 'Cornish Riviera', running non-stop from Paddington to Plymouth and then through to Penzance, the events being duly recorded in *RM*. Later the same year Swindon turned out the first of its lightweight D800 'Warships', and these 2,100/2,200hp B-Bs later became Classes 42 and 43. Some were also built by North British. Although pairs of locomotives were operated in multiple, the larger and more powerful Class 52 C-C 'Westerns' were introduced in 1961, the first being named *Western Enterprise* to rub in Swindon's way of doing things!

Each bogie of these C-C locomotives was driven by its own diesel motor through a hydraulic converter, and the power then transmitted by three sets of shafting from the main gearbox to each axle. Not surprisingly, they turned out to be

In the short-sighted rush to rid the system of steam in an artificially short space of time, BR ordered many untried, non-standard designs which turned out to be incapable of standing the test of time. The Western Region compounded the difficulty by going its own way and insisting on diesel locomotives with hydraulic, rather than electric transmission. One such type, no longer with us, was the North British-built A1A-A1A 'Warships', the first of which, No. D600 Active, *is seen approaching Shrivenham on a Bristol-Paddington demonstration run on 17th February 1958.*

very heavy on maintenance and, while there was no electric transmission, the locomotives were full of electric control circuits, so electricians were needed after all.

By the end of the 1960s BR was faced with far too many diesel locomotive designs, and set about streamlining the fleet. With the later single-engined North British Class 22s and the Beyer Peacock 'Hymek' B-Bs of 1961, the Western had just over 300 diesel-hydraulics suitable for express or mixed-traffic workings. Representing less than a fifth of the BR diesel locomotives, they were quickly singled out for withdrawal, the 'Westerns' being the last to disappear in 1977. Their work was taken over by Class 50 and Class 47 diesel-electrics, the former displaced from the West Coast route when it was electrified all the way to Glasgow in 1974.

WEST COAST ELECTRICS INTRODUCED (1959)

The Modernisation Plan proposed the electrification of the West Coast route from Liverpool and Manchester to London. The new 25kV ac system was adopted, and small batches of five different classes of electric locomotive ordered to try out various manufacturers' designs. All were built to a common performance specification, with fully-suspended traction motors, continuous ratings of 3,300hp, and capable of 90mph maxima. The first of these to be delivered, in late 1959, was Class AL1 No. E3001, which created a lot of interest in its 'electric blue' livery, with bright-metal numbers and BTC crest.

A production batch of Class AL6s (later Class 86) was subsequently ordered from Doncaster Works and the Vulcan Foundry, the first of them arriving in 1965, ready for the inauguration of services from Liverpool and Manchester to Euston the following April. Progress of the electrification and resignalling had been closely followed in our columns, and our May 1966 issue began with two articles, 'Grey Pullmans for L.M.R. Electric Services' and 'The North Western Transformed'.

O. S. Nock, in his 'P&P' article for July – 'Runs on Britain's New Railway' – gave details of the 100mph speeds which had already become commonplace, and were winning back passengers from the airlines.

Unfortunately there was a major retrogressive step with Class 86s, as their traction motors were of the nose-suspended type. Over the years that followed, their bogies were to pound the West Coast track unmercifully as they belted along, putting up maintenance costs, as well as giving

The West Coast electrification project from Liverpool and Manchester to Euston was one of the biggest civil engineering tasks undertaken by BR. New locomotives in conjunction with the scheme began being delivered in late 1959. The first off the production line was Class AL1 No. E3001, which created great interest in its 'electric blue' livery.

passengers a rough ride. There were plans to fit the class with bogies similar to the later Class 87s, built for the extension of the wires to Glasgow in 1974, but only three were so modified, being named after a trio of eminent steam locomotive engineers: Stanier, Riddles and Chapelon.

EVENING STAR COMPLETED (1960)

The last steam locomotive to be built by British Railways, No. 92220, was formally named *Evening Star* on 18th March 1960 by K. W. C. Grand, a member of the British Transport Commission, and formerly General Manager of the Western Region. The ceremony took place in 'A' Shop at Swindon, where the Class 9F 2-10-0 locomotive had been built. While the remainder of the class were unnamed and painted black, the Western Region held a competition for the last steam locomotive to be built at Swindon, with three employees suggesting the name *Evening Star*. This had first been carried by one of the broad-gauge 2-2-2s, and later by Churchward's four-cylinder 4-6-0 No. 4002. To stress the locomotive's origin, it was also finished in traditional GWR lined Brunswick green livery, with a copper-capped chimney and a brass smokebox numberplate. Commemorative plaques were also fitted under the nameplates on the smoke-deflectors.

Although nominally heavy freight locomotives, the 9Fs, with their 5ft driving wheels, were capable of a fair turn of speed, and *Evening Star* was even rostered for a main-line express turn from South Wales to Paddington.

As predicted at the time of its naming, the locomotive was preserved when it was withdrawn in 1965, but never went on display in

Another aspect of the project was the total reconstruction of Euston station, which was nearing completion when this aerial photograph was taken in October 1966.

the GWR Museum at Swindon. It was restored to working condition for the 1975 'Rail 150' Cavalcade, and subsequently operated on BR as well as various preserved lines. For some years now, it has been on display at the National Railway Museum.

MIDDLETON AND BLUEBELL RAILWAYS PRESERVED (1960)

No line has as long, or as complicated, a history as the Middleton Railway, situated in the southern outskirts of Leeds. Starting as a wooden waggon-way in 1755, it was adapted for steam locomotives using the Blenkinsop-Murray rack system in 1812. Over the years it developed into a network of lines serving the factories and mines of the area, with sections being continually opened or closed, one having been abandoned as early as 1758.

Susan Youell's article describing the line's first two centuries appeared in our April 1961 issue, by which time operations on the remaining stretch had been taken over by a preservation society. Although it beat the Bluebell Railway by carrying its first passengers – in an unpowered Swansea & Mumbles tram – on 20th June 1960, it was not until 1969 that regular passenger services began over a different stretch of the line. The idea of operating preserved trams was to be abandoned, but the 1758 Middleton Railway Trust, with the help of Leeds University Union Railway Society had, in the meanwhile, been regularly 'tripping' freight wagons between BR and factories served by the railway. No sooner had a move to Moor Road been made than the line was threatened by the construction of the South East Leeds Urban Motorway, but the line had been protected by a

The completion in March 1960 of the final BR Standard 9F class 2-10-0, No. 92220, brought to an end the glorious story of British steam locomotive manufacture, a story which for many decades had seen engines shipped from the likes of Glasgow, Leeds, Manchester and Bristol to all four corners of the Earth. To mark the sad occasion, No. 92220 was given an accolade unique to this heavy freight class . . . a name (Evening Star), a copper-capped chimney and Brunswick green passenger livery. As such, it had a short but eventful life and could often be found plying the Somerset & Dorset metals where, on 8th September 1962, it was in charge of the very last down 'Pines Express' to operate over that route.

National Trust covenant since 1960, and a tunnel had to be provided to maintain the railway connection.

One of the editorial paragraphs in our July 1960 issue read as follows:

'Bluebell Railway Progress'

Negotiations are now well advanced for the transfer of the northern end of the Southern Region line from Horsted Keynes to Culver Junction, near Lewes, to the new operating company, The Bluebell Railway Limited. A new platform, to be known as Bluebell Halt, is being constructed at Horsted Keynes, and the section to be re-opened, the 4½ miles thence to Sheffield Park, has been inspected by the Ministry of Transport. One of the 'Terrier' 0-6-0 tank engines of the former London, Brighton & South Coast Railway, built in December, 1875, as No. 55 *Stepney*, has been acquired from the Southern Region of British Railways, and was delivered at Horsted Keynes on May 17. Two passenger coaches have also been purchased. It is expected that trains will be running by the middle of next month, and every good wish for success will

be extended by railway enthusiasts to the company and the Bluebell Railway Preservation Society.'

The issue contained a photograph of the locomotive and coaches being delivered – on their own wheels – as the line then had a physical connection with BR. In our September issue came news of the reopening on 7th August, with a SECR Class P 0-6-0T 'topping and tailing' with the 'Terrier' as no run-round facilities were

available. This made the Bluebell Railway the first *standard-gauge* preserved line to operate a proper passenger service, and it has continued its successful progress ever since. The Horsted Keynes connection closed in 1963, but the Bluebell has since extended its route northwards to within two miles of the national network at East Grinstead, where platform space was made available when the BR line from London was electrified in 1987.

THE BEECHING REPORT (1963)

No other document has probably had such a dramatic effect on our whole railway system than Dr Richard Beeching's *Reshaping of British Railways*, which appeared in 1963. Introducing it in our May issue that year, the editor began:

'When the Prime Minister said, in 1960, that the railways must be of a size and pattern suited to modern conditions and prospects, and that the system must be remodelled to meet current needs, it was patently clear that, sooner or later, the railways were to be subjected to a volume of objective thinking and an exhaustive examination for replanning. The report which has just been published . . . is the outcome of much painstaking analysis and provides a revolutionary basis on which reshaping can be done.'

Thirty-odd years on, many imagine that wholesale line-closures by BR only began after the report's

The preserved railway movement had, as already recounted, started in 1950/51, but it was not until 1960 that the first standard gauge lines were rescued from the scrapman – and the race to be first to open was a close-run thing. In the end, the Middleton Railway, of Leeds, beat the Sussex-based Bluebell Railway by less than two months. Left: Crowds flock to the Bluebell Railway's Sheffield Park station to witness the newly-preserved line's first train, hauled by ex-LBSCR 'Terrier' 0-6-0T No. 55 Stepney, on 7th August 1960. Below: Very early days on the Middleton as the preserved railway's ex-LMSR Hunslet 0-6-0 diesel shunter John Alcock *is passed by an ex-GNR J50 0-6-0T on a train for Middleton Colliery.*

publication, but they had been in progress since the early fifties. Dr Beeching made 15 main recommendations, which were strongly inter-dependent. He considered that, 'If the whole plan is implemented with vigour, . . . much (though not necessarily all) of the Railways' deficit should be eliminated by 1970.'

Many of his proposals were positive in nature, such as co-ordinating suburban trains with bus services, and the railway parcels service with the Post Office, as well as increasing block-train movements of coal. Inter-city services were to be improved and routes rationalised, and the 'liner train' concept (containerisation) developed. Replacement of steam by diesel traction should be continued, up to a requirement of 'at least 3,750 to 4,250 locomotives', of which 1,698 were already in service, with another 950 on order.

One of the 'cuts' pinpointed was the vast fleet of passenger vehicles which made only a few journeys each year at peak periods. There were then 6,000 coaches which were used on no more than 18 occasions a year, a third of them venturing out of the sidings for less than ten trips annually. To put this into perspective, today's East Coast InterCity 225 fleet consists of just 315 passenger vehicles.

Dr Beeching also recommended the discontinuation of many stopping passenger services, and the closure of many small stations, and these were to have the greatest impact. The traffic-costing exercises he introduced showed how unprofitable many of these were, and another recommendation was to reduce the amount of uneconomic freight traffic by closing small goods stations and increasing charges. Wagon numbers had been decreased from 1.2million in 1946 to 850,000 by 1963, but a further 350,000 were recommended for scrapping in the next three years. (In 1995 the BR total was down to just 13,379).

While most of the report's detailed closure recommendations took place, a number of those routes are still operating as we approach the millennium. One of these is the Central Wales line, which cynics say goes through more marginal parliamentary constituencies than any other! While on a purely costing basis many of these services were undoubtedly uneconomic, thinking at that time overlooked the 'network effect'. If you close a feeder route, many of its users prefer to drive all the way to their destination, rather than to the railhead where they had previously transferred to the main-line train. The report specifically recommended the

In 1963 the Beeching Report was published, heralding the end of the line for so many rural branches, duplicated routes and stopping trains. By the following year, wholesale closures were under way and Railway Magazine's 'Panorama' picture pages during the mid-sixties were seldom free of 'last train' photographs. On 2nd May 1964, the last day of passenger services, Brush Type 2 No. D5800 approaches Wellingborough London Road with the 5.5pm train from Northampton Castle to Peterborough East. J. A. Powell

modification (down-grading) of passenger services over the East Coast route north of Newcastle, but for some years now this has been handling more InterCity passengers than the West Coast line north of Carlisle. Full account was not taken of the lack of a level playing-field between road and rail transport, nor was it seen that governments the world over would be able to persuade taxpayers to balance this with financial support for rail services.

FLYING SCOTSMAN PRESERVED (1963)

The 10am 'Special Scotch Express' began leaving King's Cross in 1862, and later became known as the 'Flying Scotsman.' The title did not become official until the 1923 Grouping, when the LNER also gave the same name to the third of Gresley's A1 Pacifics, No. 1472 (later No. 4472). For the next twelve years, *Flying Scotsman* was the company's 'star' locomotive, being exhibited at the British Empire Exhibition at Wembley, as well as pioneering long non-stop runs, which culminated in the inaugural such working from London to Edinburgh in 1928. It later became the first British

locomotive to reach an authenticated 100mph, on a special run in November 1934.

By 1962, with the 'Deltics' in service on the East Coast route, the writing was on the wall for the LNER Pacifics, and Alan Pegler, a Retford businessman and member of the Eastern Region Board, decided to preserve *Flying Scotsman*. A deal was struck, and on 14th January 1963 the locomotive, by then A3 class No. 60103, was rostered for its last BR run on the 1.15pm to Leeds. Alan was on the footplate, and the event received worldwide coverage, but some of the reports were somewhat garbled. One, in a New Zealand paper, showed the latest 'Deltic'-hauled 'Flying Scotsman' train, which Alan was said to have purchased, lock, stock and barrel!

Alan Pegler had a unique agreement as the first owner of a preserved express locomotive capable of running over BR, and the locomotive worked many specials throughout the country, the most noteworthy being the 40th anniversary non-stop run from King's Cross to Edinburgh on 1st May 1968. By then, steam on BR had almost finished, so Alan looked at the possibilities of running his locomotive elsewhere. The idea was developed to

Yes, Railway Magazine *ran railtours too! The shed staff at Southall fit the 'Welsh Mystery Flyer' headboard to preserved A3 No. 4472* Flying Scotsman *before a 'mystery tour' of the South Wales Valleys on 9th October 1965. Unfortunately the Pacific, which was to have worked the train from Paddington as far as Cardiff, failed at Swindon on the outward journey and was relieved by 'Hymek' diesel-hydraulic No. D7089.*

which 430 passengers each paid an unbelievably high fare (for those days) of 15 guineas (£15.75), ran on Sunday, 11th August. For the 314-mile round trip from Liverpool Lime Street, four different locomotives were used. LMS Class 5 No. 45110 worked the first leg along the original Liverpool & Manchester route to Manchester Victoria, where 'Britannia' No. 70013 *Oliver Cromwell* came on for the run to Carlisle over Ais Gill. The return working by the same route was in the hands of two more Class 5s, Nos 44871 and 44781, with the Pacific running light-engine behind them, *en route* to Norfolk for preservation. Hundreds lined the track throughout, many photographing the event, and a selection of their historic shots formed the 'Panorama' section of our October issue. The August issue had included R. J. Dibden's poem 'Steam', which perhaps summed up many readers' reactions to what appeared to be the final act in the story of steam motive power.

It was, however, necessary to qualify any references to BR's last steam train, by adding the words 'Main Line', as the Vale of Rheidol continued its seasonal services behind steam until the line was sold a couple of decades later. Thanks to some effective lobbying in which H. P. Bulmer, the Hereford cider company, was particularly involved, little more than three years passed before No. 6000 *King George V* reappeared on the 'Return to Steam' specials. Since then many privately-owned locomotives have operated over

use it to haul special exhibition coaches across the United States to boost British exports, and the locomotive left Liverpool in September 1969. The first test run took place in October, the locomotive having been fitted with a cow-catcher, bell and headlight to meet American requirements.

From then until mid-1972, the A3 criss-crossed the North American continent, but industrial support had been small and, with finance running out, the whole train was put into store at an army base. Creditors began to gather, and W. H. (Bill) McAlpine (now The Hon. Sir William McAlpine Bt.) sent George Hinchcliffe to California on a rescue mission. In January 1973, the locomotive was shipped back to Liverpool, where it set off, under its own steam, to Derby Works for overhaul. In mid-July it moved to the Paignton & Kingswear line, where it spent the summer, before hauling a series of steam specials over BR. In the years that followed, the locomotive has worked on many different preserved lines, as well as over BR.

A second overseas trip began in 1988, this time to Australia, where one of the specials hauled by *Flying Scotsman* set a new non-stop record of 422 miles between Parkes and Broken Hill. Since 1963 news of the locomotive has never been absent from the columns of *Railway Magazine* for long,

and it featured on the front cover for September 1993, in its latest guise as No. 60103 in BR Brunswick green and fitted once again with a double-chimney – just as it had been when purchased for preservation 30 years earlier!

A new chapter was about to begin as this was being written, following the announcement of its purchase by Dr Tony Marchington.

END OF STEAM ON BR'S MAIN LINES (1968)

Although the Modernisation Plan in 1955 indicated that BR's steam fleet still had many years to run, and new locomotives were built up to 1960, the difficulties of obtaining locomotive staff and good quality coal accelerated the withdrawal of steam motive power. The change-over was carried out area by area, with the final bastion being in the North West, and by early 1968 the writing was finally on the wall. Our February issue referred to 'abolition of steam traction from passenger trains on British Railways was almost complete by early November, and only a handful of regular steam turns then existed'. A few months later it was announced that the final trains would run on the first Sunday in early August, and several societies took the opportunity to charter specials that day.

BR's own commemorative special, for

The mid and late-sixties were punctuated by numerous 'Farewell to Steam' specials, culminating on 11th August 1968 with the last of them all, the 'Fifteen Guinea Special'. The Western Region, however, had (officially) said goodbye to steam on 27th November 1965 when 'Castle' class 4-6-0 No. 7029 Clun Castle *ran from Paddington to Swindon, Bristol, Gloucester, Cheltenham and back to Swindon. It is pictured at Gloucester Eastgate.*

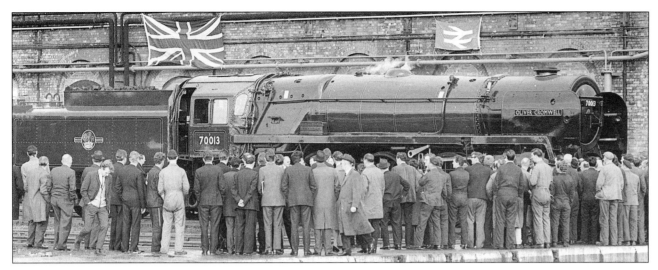

For Crewe Works, the end of steam came on 2nd February 1967 when 'Britannia' Pacific No. 70013 Oliver Cromwell *left the works as the last non-preserved steam locomotive to be repaired by British Rail. After participating in the 'Fifteen Guinea Special' the next year, it was, of course, preserved itself.* John Hillier

One of the greatest success stories of the last quarter of the century has concerned the 'Inter City 125' (or High Speed Train' as it is often referred to). The wide route availability of these 125mph diesel-electric sets has seen members of the class working to Penzance, Inverness, Aberdeen, Bournemouth, Holyhead and almost all points in between. Originating from a Class 252 prototype unveiled in 1972, the Class 253 (Western Region) and 254 (Eastern Region) production versions made their debuts in 1976 and 1978 respectively and have since made 'HST' a household word. HSTs can now also be seen on the West Coast Main Line and this example, led by power car No. 43051, is seen at Milton Keynes Central.

more and more routes, with *Railway Magazine* being involved with Days Out Ltd in three memorable 'time trial' runs with Pacifics over Shap in Autumn 1995.

BARRY SCRAPYARD (1968-1990)

Over a period of thirty years, thousands of railway enthusiasts made pilgrimages to Woodham's scrap yard at Barry Docks in South Wales. In all, 288 locomotives were sent there, making what most expected was to be their last journey,

The current size of the preservation movement is due in no small way to what has become known as the 'Barry phenomenon'. If it hadn't been for South Wales scrap merchants, Woodham Bros, who delayed the cutting of no fewer than 213 steam locomotives to enable enthusiasts to buy them, many of today's steam lines would have a paucity of motive power, if indeed they had ever got off the ground at all. In this cab-top view taken on 28th May 1967, some of the 200-plus engines are seen lined-up in the rows which were to become a familiar sight to thousands of enthusiasts during the next 20 years.

but only 76 of them were actually demolished.

Dai and Billy Woodham were by no means the only scrap dealers to buy withdrawn locomotives. They were however, also involved in cutting up a stream of withdrawn wagons, during which the locomotives were left to moulder gently in the sea air. As a result, preservation interests were able to marshall the financial and physical resources to rescue them. No less than 213 locomotives were bought by individuals or societies, most being intended for ultimate restoration to steaming condition. Some were purchased for spares, while Rebuilt 'Merchant Navy' No. 35029 *Ellerman Lines* was sectioned to go on display for the opening of the National Railway Museum in 1975.

The first Barry locomotive to be purchased was ex-LMS 4F 0-6-0 No. 43924 in 1968, and the final departure was the GWR Collett 2-8-0 No. 3845, which left in November 1990. For three decades references to the yard were never absent long from our columns, and Peter Nicholson contributed an article to the January 1990 issue, describing the saga's final chapter. Some 120 people gathered to see the last locomotive depart, the event enabling many of those closely involved to recount their parts in the story, Dai Woodham included.

EAST COAST ELECTRIFICATION COMPLETED (1991)

The East Coast route as far as York had been listed for possible electrification in the 1955 Modernisation Plan. However, it was not until 1984 that the go-ahead was given, but the scheme

then covered the whole of the line to Edinburgh. Almost exactly seven years later, on 8th July 1991, the full electric service was introduced between King's Cross, Edinburgh and Glasgow, the Edinburgh–Carstairs stretch having been added on in 1989. Some electric services had begun much earlier, reaching Huntingdon in November 1986, Peterborough the following May, and, from September 1989 the 'Yorkshire Pullman' from Leeds had been worked by the first of the new InterCity 225s.

Originally it was intended to use Class 89 Co-Co locomotives and new MkIII coaches with sliding doors, but the plans were changed to use 6,300hp Class 91 Bo-Bos hauling coaches of a new design (MkIVs), with a Driving Van Trailer at the other end. The new trains were designed for a maximum of 140mph, but the route's signalling would need up-grading to permit this speed to be used in everyday service. However, when the special launch run to Edinburgh took place in September 1991, over 40 per cent of the route was specially cleared for a 140 maximum. The writer was the official timekeeper for the journey, and the 3hr 29min schedule was kept, *to the second –* an overall average of nearly 113mph.

Even with the normal 125mph limit, 110+mph start-to-stop averages have been scheduled at the southern end of the line. In the summer of 1995 it was being advertised as Britain's

Fastest Railway, with the morning 'Yorkshire Pullman' averaging more than 96mph from Leeds to King's Cross, inclusive of its Wakefield stop. A run with invited passengers in June that year reached a record speed of 154mph at two separate locations.

EUROSTARS AND THE CHANNEL TUNNEL (1994)

On 14th November 1994 the first public Eurostar services began, taking passengers between England and France through the Channel Tunnel. In May the following year some 200,000 people were carried on the London–Paris route alone.

Proposals for an Anglo–French 'Fixed Link' substantially predate the start of this magazine, and 15 years before our first issue hit the news-stands, the first construction attempts had been called off because of military opposition. In 1974 a second attempt was abandoned, but the end of 1987 saw the start of Eurotunnel's private-sector project which was to lead to the completion of the 33-mile link. Both from the ownership and construction points of view, it has throughout been an Anglo-French operation.

The progress of what was to become one of the world's largest-ever civil engineering projects was closely followed in *Railway Magazine*, and the interest generated by a October 1989 supplement prompted a monthly 'Channel Tunnel Update' until the official inauguration by Queen Elizabeth

II and President Mitterand in May 1994. That event, in turn, was marked by the publication of a souvenir issue of the magazine.

As well as Eurotunnels' own frequent Le Shuttle trains conveying accompanied road vehicles between the terminals at Folkestone and Calais, the tunnel takes through passenger and freight trains operated by the national railways on the two sides of the Channel. The lorry shuttles began first, followed by the international freight trains. The Eurostars were the first passenger trains passed to use the tunnel on a commercial basis, and finally came the car-carrying shuttles.

No other stretch of railway in the world has been subjected to such rigorous safety requirements, which increased the cost, lengthened the construction time and delayed the commissioning. The culmination of this forced Eurotunnel in the autumn of 1995 to suspend its interest payments to the banks for 18 months, providing yet another opportunity for media speculation about its future.

The quarter-mile long Eurostars are probably the most complex trains in the world, being capable of operating from the different British, Belgian and French electrification systems, and reaching speeds of 186mph on the French high-speed lines. After several proposals for a high-speed link from London to the Tunnel had been turned down, proposals were still going through parliament in 1996 for one from

St Pancras to Folkestone, to be constructed by London & Continental Railways Ltd. It is unlikely to open before 2002.

PRIVATISATION (1994-)

In the 1980s, under Prime Minister Margaret Thatcher, many nationalised organisations were returned to the private sector. They markedly improved their business performance, albeit with considerable reductions in staff and some public annoyance at profits and the salaries paid to directors. British Railways, which had been formed from the four Grouping companies during the post-war spate of nationalisation, was clearly an organisation that right-wing politicians wished to return to the private sector, but the complexity of the operation put it well down the political agenda.

The Government's desire for privatisation was in spite of the clear successes of sectorisation, which included InterCity operating without any government subsidy, making it unique in the western world.

There were suggestions for the privatisation of BR as a whole, but the 'unbundling' proposals that finally emerged had all the marks of the civil service. Several new bureaucracies were formed, and the ownership of the infrastructure (and property portfolio) was transferred to Railtrack, a separate company, the shares of which were sold in May 1996. All the rolling stock was sold to leasing companies (ROSCOs), and they, as well as Railtrack, raise charges for their use from the 25 passenger Train Operating Companies which were to be franchised. To get any private-sector takers for most of the businesses that carry passengers, they require subsidies, meaning they are still not free from ultimate control by the Government.

The split took effect on 1st April 1994, but subsequent progress was far slower than originally announced. The first big sales were the three ROSCOs (for £1.8billion) in the autumn of 1995, and at the time of writing, eight of the passenger operating companies had been franchised. Meanwhile the fragmentisation of the system produced numerous disadvantages for the users, examples having already been given as early as April 1994 in an article by Nick Pigott.

RM has regularly covered the changing privatisation scene, beginning with general articles in 1992 and delving into the details as they occurred. Everyone, except perhaps those in the road lobby, hopes our railway system will benefit from the changes, but the jury is still out on that one.

A prestigious and long overdue civil engineering project – the electrification of the East Coast Main Line from London to Edinburgh and Glasgow – was completed in 1991. The section to Leeds had, however, been energised in 1989 and the first of the Class 91 locomotives built to power the InterCity 225 trains, No. 91001 Swallow, *stands at King's Cross with the 07.50 'Yorkshire Pullman' to Leeds on 5th January 1990.* Chris Wilson

THE CHANGING ENTHUSIAST SCENE

During the century since the first issue of *Railway Magazine* was printed, the enthusiasts' scene has changed considerably and, at the same time, their interests are now catered for far more extensively. The aim of this section is to give an overview of the developments that have taken place.

Prior to the 1890s, there was little or no 'framework' which those who were interested in the subject could use to further their knowledge. The availability of *Locomotive Magazine* and then the wider-ranging *Railway Magazine* provided important sources of information but, although the latter's cover price of 6d (2½p) does not sound very high, it was effectively something for which only the middle-classes had sufficient disposable income to afford. (In 1909 Bill Hoole, whose speed exploits with the King's Cross A4s were to endear him to enthusiasts in the 1950s, was glad to earn extra 'bonce' by repairing guard's lamps at 6d a time!).

How many of those who bought the magazine were 'closet enthusiasts' is not known, but it certainly prospered. Clergy were, no doubt, among them. Not only was the Rev. J. W. Scott an initial contributor, but the fact that other 'men of the cloth' were well-known for their railway interest caused Ealing Studios to make the local vicar the volunteer fireman of *Lion* when they shot the film *The Titfield Thunderbolt*.

Mention must, of course, be made of that superb railway photographer, the Rev. Eric Treacy, who died on the lineside at Appleby, photographing his favourite locomotive *Evening Star*, and to the Rev. Wilbert Awdry, whose Thomas the Tank Engine books gave railways an appeal to children. 'Thomas' merchandising has become a huge business and has been picked up in a big way by preservation societies with 'Thomas' weekends.

Eric Treacy finished his ministry as Bishop of Wakefield, but it appears we now have an even more exalted churchman with a railway interest. For Dr David Hope, in the address following his installation as Archbishop of York in December 1995, referred to his first visit to the city as a youngster and recalled the fact that he had been more interested in *Mallard* in the engine sheds than the tomb of a former archbishop in the Minster.

Whether or not all self-respecting young boys at that time wanted 'to be an engine driver when they grew up', that ambition had certainly developed by the 1930s, as the writer knows! A couple of decades later still, when he had begun to write and lecture about railways, it was interesting to note how many wives, learning of his interest, promptly commented, somewhat *sotto voce*, that their husbands were interested too! Richard Marsh (formerly a Labour Minister of Transport), in his days as Chairman of British Railways, once referred to the fact that, in addition to the 100,000 or so then employed by the railways, some 20-odd million others in the country (ie the whole of the male population) also had views on how the railways should be run! Even today the head of one British airline reads *Railway Magazine*, and there are persistent rumours that a Chancellor of the Exchequer used to organise rail tours in his younger days!

The London-based Railway Club was founded in 1899, 'for those interested, professionally or otherwise, in Railways and Locomotives', but in 1909 the Stephenson Locomotive Society (SLS) became the first nation-wide railway enthusiast organisation to be started. Interestingly, it subsequently helped catalyse the formation of the Institution of Locomotive Engineers. The SLS also became the first private society to preserve a steam locomotive when it obtained the London, Brighton & South Coast 0-4-2 *Gladstone* in 1927, and two years earlier had started its monthly *Journal*. In 1928, the Railway Correspondence & Travel Society was formed, and was later able to boast the largest membership of any railway society. Railway societies were also formed at several universities, that at Cambridge at one time organising 'driving days' for its members on a branch line, while the annual dinner of the Oxford society used to be held in a dining car between Swindon and the university city.

It was after World War II when things started to change in a big way. In 1942 a booklet, *The ABC of Southern Locomotives – A Complete list of all Southern Railway Engines in Service*, was produced by Ian Allan. Although similar books had existed earlier, such as *Great Western Railway Engines – Names, Numbers, Types and Classes*, available from the Railway Publishing Co. in 1935, it was Ian Allan's comprehensive and annual pocket-sized editions which were to launch the massive hobby of 'trainspotting'. So large were the numbers that descended on BR at weekends and during school holidays that some stations confined them to corrals, while others banned them altogether. In the late 1970s and 1980s, however, BR had its own Great Rail Club which subsequently changed its name to Railriders Club. Members received vouchers giving discounts for train journeys, which enabled the writer's teen-aged son to do an afternoon's spotting at Leeds, travelling from York and back for the princely sum of 4p!

The spotters' ABCs were the foundation of the Ian Allan publishing empire, and just after the war the company brought out its first magazine, *Trains Illustrated*. E. L. Lake had started *Railways* in 1939, and its name changed to *Railway World* in 1952, but it subsequently fell on hard times and was taken over by Ian Allan in 1960. This enabled Geoffrey Freeman Allen to redirect *Trains Illustrated* at professional railwaymen, changing the name to *Modern Railways*.

During the Grouping era, the four main-line companies all produced books of various sorts. The first part of MacDermot's *History of the Great Western Railway* appeared in 1927 and, together with Tomlinson's *The North Eastern Railway – Its Rise and Development*, jointly published by two firms in 1914, they still provide authoritative accounts of those railways' early days. In 1936, the Southern Railway produced Dendy Marshall's *A History of the Southern Railway*. However, it was not until two decades later that the spate of histories covering various pre-Grouping railways began to appear, published by several different firms.

In addition to their advertising material, some of the 'Big Four' produced books about their famous trains, or what could be seen from them, examples being the LNER's *The Flying Scotsman* and *On Either Side*, and the Southern's *ACE* by S. P. B. Mais. The GWR published a series of books by W. G. Chapman '*For Boys of All Ages*', which were extremely popular. Within seven months of the first appearance of the 232-page *Cheltenham Flyer* in 1934, they had printed 30,000 copies, selling at one shilling each (5p).

Since the 1960s, thousands of railway books have been produced, these being of two main types. Initially they could perhaps be loosely described as historical or descriptive accounts, with a few illustrations, but later, many photographic albums were put on the market. There was a tendency for these to be dismissed by some as having little or no historical importance, but it may be that their real significance is only now becoming more apparent. It took a long time for industrial archaeologists to accept that photographs were a valid prime source of information, and it could well be that they, and future historians, will find that invaluable data lurks in the background of well-captioned railway photographs.

The start of the preservation movement in the 1950s produced a major new slant for railway enthusiasm, providing a whole new set of people with the opportunity to get their hands dirty, and experience the satisfaction of restoring part of our railway heritage to working order. By 1996, there were more than 50 standard gauge operating railways, 50 steam centres, 30 museums and numerous narrow gauge lines. Although there have been many dire warnings about too many operating lines chasing too few customers, it is estimated that they now carry some 9 million passengers a year, and there have been few 'failures'.

Each of these societies nevertheless faces two major tasks, the first being the constant need to attract new young members to take on the role of carrying the torch. They cannot exist simply by preserving a minor line exactly as it was in the 1950s and Andrew Scott, the Head of the National Railway Museum, pointed out in an Institute of Railway Studies lecture in 1995 that they are actually in a state of change. This is because their continued existence depends on becoming a microcosm of a full-blown steam railway, albeit with a disproportionately large ratio of locomotives to coaches, rather than a sleepy branch along which trains occasionally pottered, serving the transport needs of a rural community.

There was considerable interest when the LNER Railway Museum at York reopened after the war, but few would have imagined that a little over a quarter of a century later, a queue four deep and several hundred yards long would be waiting to enter the new National Railway Museum there, as soon as the formal opening by the Duke of Edinburgh in 1975 had been completed. It was not only remarkable that the country could afford such a prestigious establishment, but that it attracted a large audience of all ages, and one that was not predominantly male.

Some of the preservation societies can boast extremely large memberships, the Festiniog Railway's at one time rivalling that of a country-wide heritage organisation, before the latter got down to serious marketing. Most preservation organisations also publish their own newsletters, which has added considerably to the output of printed railway material. There are also several societies devoted to the study of particular pre-Grouping railways with publications describing aspects of their companies' history.

The 1970s, '80s and '90s also saw a considerable increase in the availability of commercial railway magazines, such as the two on modern traction which had been started in 1981 and 1994 by Peter Kelly and Nick Pigott respectively, as referred to in their biographical details. Others deal in depth with historical matters, or the Continental scene.

The past century has also seen the publication of several significant part-works on railways. F. A. Talbot edited *Railway Wonders of the World* for Cassell just before World War I, and the title was reused by the Amalgamated Press in the 1930s, Cecil J. Allen acting as consulting editor to Clarence Winchester. In the early 1970s, New English Library published *Trains & Railways*, under the editorship of John Adams and Pat Whitehouse, who had also been responsible for the long-running 'Railway Roundabout' series of programmes for BBC Television. The most recent railway part-work has been Eaglemoss Publications' *The World of Trains*, which ran for 135 issues in 1991-1994.

The final years of steam on British main lines produced a great surge of interest, with society memberships soaring and people flocking to make visits and special journeys. In view of the widespread antipathy to diesel and electric traction at that time, there was much speculation whether railway enthusiast interest would continue beyond 1968. While numbers did decrease, the send-off given to the 'Deltics' in 1982 showed that modern motive power had acquired its followers and preservation enthusiasts.

So, how has the actual enthusiast changed during the last century? To start off with, back in 1897, he was known as a 'Railwayac', with 'Railway Enthusiast' and 'Railfan' only emerging later. In the heyday of the Ian Allan ABCs, 'Trainspotter' became the usual term, followed by 'Gricer' for the number collector, being an irregular plural of someone who grouses. In recent years the media, apparently as part of their general attitude of trying to rubbish any occupation that does not involve the media, suddenly decided to call railway enthusiasts 'Anoraks', although there are many more wearers of such garments at any football match than on a railway station.

Some academic historians consider that material from periodicals such as *Railway Magazine* or its competitors should not be used as a basis for academic research, but other historians disagree. Professor Colin Divall, the new head of the Institute of Railway Studies at the National Railway Museum, has said that 'the news reported today in such magazines is tomorrow's history'.

There can be little doubt that the informed public perception of what the railways have been doing at any period during the last century can be appreciated better from our columns, rather than the material in any public record office. With all the rapid changes taking place with computer technology, would it be too much to hope that, for the millennium, we might have a full index of all 146 volumes of *Railway Magazine* on CD ROM?

As we closed for press with this book, public and professional opinion on the merits and demerits of privatisation was still sharply divided, but one of the more positive aspects from an enthusiast's point of view has been the rehabilitation of locomotive types generally considered defunct. One such example was the rebuilding at the Loughborough works of Brush Traction of a small fleet of Class 20s for use by Direct Rail Services on behalf of British Nuclear Fuels Ltd. Underlining the blurring of the edges between former BR operations and preserved railways, the ex-works diesel-electrics were taken to the privately-operated Great Central Railway for test-running, and No. 20302 is seen at Rothley in the company of preserved classmate No. D8098 on 11th October 1995. John Stretton

A Celebration in Art
by
The Guild of Railway Artists

Last days of Steam at Rose Grove

Peter Annable, GRA
Oils. 24in x 18in (610mm x 457mm)

PETER ANNABLE, GRA

Peter Annable was born in Nottingham and has lived most of his life in Nottinghamshire.

After two years at Mansfield Art College, he took up a career in graphic design. Since 1987 he has worked as a freelance artist, taking on graphic design and illustration work for industry as well as private commissions.

He works in both oils and watercolours, the latter being his preferred medium. He enjoys painting from nature and believes the spontaneity and freshness of sketching in the countryside is an invaluable experience when it comes to producing studio work.

His railway subjects usually depict the final years of steam with the muck, grime and atmosphere associated with this period. He also made a number of visits to sketch and paint at Barry scrapyard.

Other than railway subjects, he is a keen landscape painter and prints of his landscapes of Britain are widely available throughout the country.

Dockyard Shunter

Peter Annable, GRA
Watercolour. 4.5in x 6.5in (114mm x 165mm)

B. R. Standard at Barry

Peter Annable, GRA
Oils. 7.75in x 13.5in (198mm x 333mm)

The Forth Bridge

John Austin, GRA
Oils. 26in x 39in (660mm x 990mm)
The Scottish entertainer Billy Connolly described it as the most beautiful bridge in the world. 54,000 tons of steel over 150 feet above water level, A3 class 4-6-2 No. 60103 Flying Scotsman *is dwarfed as it heads north across this great steel dinosaur.*

JOHN AUSTIN, GRA

After a diversity of occupations dominated by creative lighting design and later running a pub, a change in circumstances gave John the opportunity to realise a lifelong ambition to become an artist, specialising in steam engines.

A move to a cold 300-year old house on the banks of the River Severn at Bridgnorth, close to the Severn Valley Railway, provided a perfect inspirational environment

A large canvas depicting SR Pacific *Taw Valley* painted on site in December 1987 was displayed in The Railwayman's Arms, on the platform of Bridgnorth station, attracting much criticism by Severn Valley Railway staff and volunteers. It became painfully obvious that a greater knowledge of the subject would be required. John began working as a volunteer at Bridgnorth engine shed carrying out repairs and such tasks as boiler washouts. Many hours spent in a very close proximity to the locomotives began to pay dividends in the paintings. Pictures began to sell and commissions followed, including the Severn Valley Railway timetables and publicity posters. John joined the Guild of Railway Artists in 1991 and was successful in winning the Lawrence Hammonds Award for the Picture of the Year in 1993, 1994 and 1995.

At present John's life is dominated by long hours of painting but he is happy in the knowledge that a few pints of real ale in The Railwayman's Arms will be his reward at the end of the day.

Great Western Railway Splendour at Bewdley

John Austin, GRA
Oils 30in x 40in (760mm x 1016mm)
A scene from the preservation era – GWR preserved 'King' class 4-6-0 No. 6024 King Edward I *leaves Bewdley on an afternoon Bridgnorth to Kidderminster train on the Severn Valley Railway.*

Blues 1 Stoke City 0

John Austin, GRA
Oils. 30in x 48in (760mm x 1220mm)
On a cold damp January Saturday in the mid-1950s, a
heavy freight struggles past St Andrews Football Ground
creating a smoke screen over the pitch. Such an occasion
was recorded in Terry Essery's book Firing Days at Saltley.
That night in the Birmingham Sports Argus *the headlines*
were, 'Blues Win through the Smoke'.

Dirty Old Town

John Austin, GRA
Oils. 18in x 24in (455mm x 610mm)
Inspired in part by the Euan McColl song 'Dirty Old Town',
a Stanier 'Black 5' heads a freight through an
industrial Lancashire landscape.

A Rolling Royce Railcar

Peter Barnfield
Pen and Ink/Pencil Crayon.
9in x 13in (220mm x 320mm)

The New Multiple Aspect Signalling, Myrtle Junction, Whimshire

Peter Barnfield
Pen and Ink/Pencil Crayon.
13in x 20in (320mm x 500mm)

Fighter Pilot

Graham Beech
Oils. 20in x 30in (550mm x 760mm)

PETER BARNFIELD

Born in 1942, Peter was ejected from art classes at the age of 12, had to take up woodwork instead, and hasn't had an art lesson or cut a decent dovetail joint since! After working for 27 years in the printing industry he became a freelance graphic designer in 1986. 'Steam Pencil' and 'Whimseyrail' artwork soon ousted more mundane work however, and now accounts for most drawing board time.

Specialising in finely detailed pencil drawings of West Country railway scenes of the '50s and '60s, he also enjoys portraying his lifelong passion for bucolic light railways, often depicting the overgrown narrow gauge tracks of the Portersfoote Bunting Light Railway (PBLR) meandering through mythical Whimshire. Rolling stock for a 16mm model of this line is currently being constructed from card offcuts from picture mounts and a PBLR railcar usually finds a place amongst his displays of drawings, limited edition prints and cards at model railway exhibitions.

Based in Bristol, Peter and his wife Ginny have worked as volunteers on a number of preserved railways and also enjoy country walking, landscape photography and collecting vintage photographica.

GRAHAM BEECH

Graham Beech was born in Portsmouth where he still resides and has been a railway enthusiast since the tender age of four.

Totally self taught, he took up painting in 1974 as 'something to do' after the demise of steam on British Railways and has experimented in various media, but now paints exclusively in oils.

The painting of *Fighter Pilot* was inspired by many visits to Eastleigh Locomotive Sheds in the early 1960s with nostalgic recollections playing a major part in his subject matter.

For the past 23 years, Graham has been a full-time firefighter, currently with the Hampshire Fire and Rescue Service, and a member of the Guild of Railway Artists since 1983.

STUART BLACK

Stuart Black joined the Guild of Railway Artists as an Associate Member in 1987. He is a specialist in the field of graphic art and has become well known for his profile illustrations of locomotives and aircraft.

Born in 1955, Stuart was brought up amidst strong family connections with the railways. With much encouragement from his father, he developed a keen interest in steam locomotives from the age of four. His early enthusiasm was spurred on by the fact that his first school had its playground alongside the main line at York! He was educated at Woodbridge School in Suffolk where he received his only formal art training. He considered a career in architecture but a strong desire to fly resulted in him joining the RAF as a navigator in 1974. Since then he has flown Phantoms, F-14 Tomcats (with the US Navy) and undertaken service around the world including active duty in Saudi Arabia during the Gulf War. At the time of writing, his appointment was Officer Commanding the F3 Operational Evaluation Unit, flying Tornados from RAF Coningsby, Lincolnshire.

Stuart's artwork is a pastime that has evolved from his early association with the railways and his natural flair for precision drawing and painting. His hallmark is attention to detail; each original is painstakingly researched to ensure accuracy and authenticity. He works with drawing pens, fine brushes and gouache paints to achieve the desired effect; he does not use an airbrush. Stuart's distinctive paintings have been reproduced in many forms including prints, cards, table mats, book marks and playing cards. His illustrations have also featured in a variety of publications including railway magazines and museum guides.

GWR 'City' class 4-4-0 No. 3440 City of Truro

Stuart Black
Pen and Gouache   9in x 21in   (228mm x 520mm)
City of Truro *was one of a batch of ten 4-4-0s built at Swindon in 1903. The locomotive achieved world fame on 9th May 1904 by becoming the first locomotive to exceed a speed of 100 mph. The locomotive is now an exhibit at the National Railway Museum, York.*

LMS 'Princess Coronation' Pacific No. 6223 Princess Alice

Stuart Black
Pen and Gouache. 9in x 25in   (228mm x 635mm)
Princess Alice *was one of five locomotives built at Crewe in 1937 to haul the prestigious 'Coronation Scot' express between London and Glasgow.*

BREL/GEC Class 90 No. 90 019 Penny Black

Stuart Black
Pen and Gouache. 9in x 23in (228mm x 584mm)
Fifty Class 90 electric locomotives were built for British Rail at Crewe Works between 1987 and 1990. No. 90 019 Penny Black *wears the striking livery of Rail express systems and carries an impressive cast plate image of a Penny Black stamp.*

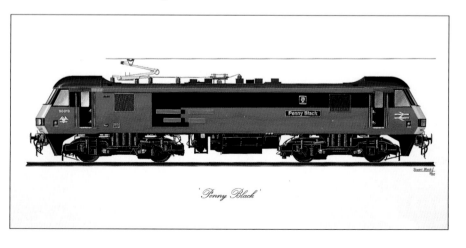

MIKE BOOTH, GRA, NDD, ATD, DA (Manc)

Mike Booth was born in Manchester where he also received an education, much of it at the Stretford End, and some at the College of Art.

Having decided not to become a studio potter, professional footballer or international playboy, Mike spent 27 years as an art teacher in Derbyshire and Nottinghamshire before taking early retirement in 1992 to concentrate on painting and poverty. He is still involved in adult education in the Mansfield and Ashfield area.

He emphasises that he is not a traditional railway buff and usually has to be told whether an engine that finds itself in the painting is a tank or a 'Britannia'.

He still paints nostalgia to commission but finds a particular fascination in preservation and renovation, finding subjects in working tank engines, station gas lamps and the detritus of railway. Surfaces provide a major source of inspiration whether it be the layers of faded paint peeling from abandoned carriages, or the effect of a blue sky reflecting in a polished crimson boiler, or the rich colours and textures of oiled or rusting metal.

Gently does it

Mike Booth, GRA
Oils. 30in x 20in (760mm x 510mm)

Anlaby Road Crossing

Eric Bottomley, GRA
Oils. 20in x 30in
(510mm x 760mm)

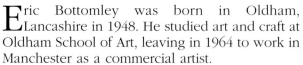

ERIC BOTTOMLEY, GRA

Eric Bottomley was born in Oldham, Lancashire in 1948. He studied art and craft at Oldham School of Art, leaving in 1964 to work in Manchester as a commercial artist.

In 1974 he moved to Dorset, continuing as a freelance artist/illustrator which enabled him to devote more time to oil painting. Two years later he took up fine art full time from his studio in Wimborne Minster.

Eric's subjects are mostly of a nostalgic nature, depicting the age of steam railways, vintage transport and more recently the Victorian and Edwardian era.

He joined the Guild of Railway Artists in 1979, later to become a Full Member.

In the field of genre painting, Eric's use of models wearing period costume and his painstaking research into town and country life from photographs and books help him to produce an accurate study of life in days gone by. A great deal of Eric's work is privately commissioned but, in order to be more self indulgent in his subject matter, he has, over the last years, staged one-man exhibitions.

Eric now lives and works in the village of Much Marcle, near Ledbury, Herefordshire.

The Wicker Arch, Sheffield

Eric Bottomley, GRA
Oils. 20in x 30in (510mm x 760mm)

Dean Single below Dartmoor, near South Brent, 1913

Gerald Broom, GRA
Acrylic. 16in x 24in (406mm x 610mm)

GERALD BROOM, GRA

Gerald has firm views on art and railways. Born in the Heart of England, he believes the craftmanship of traditional art around the turn of the century has never been surpassed.

He sees railways as a romantic extension, in a unique period of history that, through its social and commercial need was, in concept, altruistic. The steam engine, fire, water, air, was such a demonstration of elemental control, enabling it to blend with nature and humanity on a spiritual and heroic scale. "If only Alma-Tadema or the Pre-Raphaelites had painted trains!"

Having no formal artistic training, Gerald Broom developed from "Steam and trucks and Rock 'n' Roll" to become professional in 1968; his aim to "simply present an illustration of a scene before colour film".

He works in many mediums, preferring the railway in its natural environment, though his dedication to locomotives is found in the engineering side of railway preservation. He also paints various aspects of the traditional and historic scene, and has recently been working on a battle panorama of the English archers at Agincourt.

***Tebay Troughs. LMS. 1935. 6100* Royal Scot**

Gerald Broom, GRA
Acrylic. 20in x 28in (508mm x 711mm)

Clifton Road Junction, Rugby 1920. LNWR

Gerald Broom, GRA
Acrylic. 22in x 42in (558mm x 1067mm)

The Royal Train, Killiekrankie, 1928

Gerald Broom, GRA
Acrylic. 22in x 32in   (558mm x 813mm)

Morning at St Quentin

George Busby, GRA
Watercolour. 7.5in x 11in (190mm x 280mm)

Is it worth it?

George Busby, GRA
Watercolour. 9in x 13in (230mm x 330mm)

GEORGE BUSBY, GRA, MCSD, RBSA, FRSA

George Busby was born in Birmingham in 1926 and still lives and works in the West Midlands. For many years he was engaged as a graphic designer and illustrator. In 1978 he finally decided to leave the advertising world to take up painting as a full-time artist.

Working mainly in watercolour and gouache, he covers a variety of subjects, but the industrial scene remains his favourite, with railways in particular.

He has been commissioned to illustrate calendars by many leading companies including British Gas, British Waterways and Amoco Oil Company. He was also represented in a series of calendars entitled 'British Watercolours' and has published greetings cards featuring his paintings.

Exhibiting regularly in galleries in London, the Midlands, Cumbria and North Wales, his work is included in the National Library of Wales and in numerous private collections.

In addition to membership of the Guild of Railway Artists, George Busby is a Member of the Chartered Society of Designers, a Member of the Royal Birmingham Society of Artists and a Fellow of the Royal Society of Arts.

Interlaken West

George Busby, GRA
Watercolour. 7.5in x 11in (190mm x 280mm)

Tyseley Tea Break

George Busby, GRA
Watercolour. 19.5in x 25.5in (500mm x 650mm)

DAVID CHARLESWORTH, GRA

David Charlesworth began drawing at an age too early to even remember, started painting with oils when eight years old and completed his first 'official' commission when only 15. He is still one of the country's 'younger' artists, and one of the very few of his generation with over 25 years continuous experience producing and selling paintings and illustrations.

David Charlesworth specialises in working to specific customer requirements for companies as well as individual clients, with originals and prints being despatched as far as Australia and USA.

Trained as a litho artist in the graphics trade, David uses his background training and education to the full, producing graphics and illustration work for a variety of customers under his trading name, Notions by Design. As a working artist this makes computers an integral part of his working environment and David now owns two very powerful PC-based graphic systems and produces most of his commercial artwork on them, combining the strengths of traditional training and experience with the latest technology.

A Full Member of the Guild of Railway Artists, David's work is not confined to railway subjects. The breadth of his experience has covered every subject and medium. A competent photographer, he is also co-author and producer of a colourful book on India, entitled *India, No problem Sahib*, and the illustrator and designer of *Chwedlau – Ffestiniog Fables*, produced for the Festiniog Railway Company.

Electra *at Dunford Bridge*

David Charlesworth, GRA
Oils. 16in x 20in (410mm x 510mm)
"You had to stand on tiptoes to get this view over the high bridge parapet. I loved this railway and its unique locomotives, but looking back, as always, I never found the time to visit the tunnel as often as I should. One memorable day in February 1981, Totley Tunnel on the Sheffield to Manchester route, was again closed for repairs. The services were diverted over the Woodhead route, and even with a reversal at Sheffield requiring the driver to walk the full length of the train, Manchester was reached 10 minutes quicker – what progress!"

Patriot 45509 **The Derbyshire Yeomanry**

David Charlesworth, GRA
Watercolour. 8in x 10in (200mm x 250mm)
"LMS Patriots – I barely remember these, though would have seen them. So what, we can still enjoy re-creating the scenes but I wish I could recall how I produced the colour used for the coupling rods!"

MATTHEW COUSINS

Born in Hitchin in 1953 within sight and sound of the Great Northern main line, Matthew has always been interested in railways and has, from an early age, been interested particularly in drawing and painting transport subjects. The power and speed of steam trains, aircraft and cars has always impressed him, together with the tranquillity of the railway scene and how it had mellowed into the landscape when there were no trains actually passing.

The art of railway posters has also had a profound influence on Matthew, and he is grateful that some enlightened souls were prepared to get such good artists producing work in the 1950s and '60s. His own work has been largely moulded by the requests made on him to produce paintings by commission or other art work such as pub signs and poster work that challenges him to work in different media, from watercolour and line drawing through to enamels.

Matthew now lives near to and regularly works on the Bluebell Railway, and has been on the footplate roster since the late 1980s enjoying the hard work and the exhilarating ride on the engines, particularly now that the line has extended through the tunnel.

Bluebell Time

Matthew Cousins Gouache. 14in x 11.5in (355mm x 292mm)

Transatlantic Super Power – Class 59 at Reading

Norman Elford, GRA
Alkyd. 24in x 36in
(670mm x 910mm)

NORMAN ELFORD, NDD, GRA, ATD

Norman Elford was born in Portsmouth but it wasn't until he spent the war years with an aunt in Reading that his real interest in railways developed. The GWR line between Reading West and Tilehurst Junction marked the bottom of his aunt's garden and he remembers many an hour spent by the main line and wandering around the 'Castles', 'Halls' and the huge variety of goods locomotives on Reading shed. He also remembers the visual shock of seeing one of the first USA 2-8-0s simmering at the end of the garden and recalls, that to English eyes, it looked like a plumber's shop on wheels!

After a long career in teaching, Norman began to paint seriously in 1978 and has held several one-man exhibitions, two of these being at the prestigious Stroud Arts Festival. He has had his work published as greetings cards and calendars and has designed decorative plates for both Spode and Royal Doulton. He works largely to commission, his customers favouring his sharp and detailed use of acrylics but he also works in oil and alkyd with the same attention to detail.

Although he retains an affection for steam he confesses to a growing interest in the current railway scene with its exciting new shapes and colours, and to the human interest element present at busy stations.

Southern Suburbia

Barry Freeman, GRA
Oils. 20in x 30in (508mm x 762mm)

BARRY FREEMAN, BA, GRA, FRSA

Barry was born in Northampton in 1937. Following ten years service in the Royal Navy and several more in the electronics and aviation industries he taught drawing and painting for 18 years before becoming a full time artist, in 1989.

An avid railway enthusiast since early childhood, his combined love of art and railways is reflected in the detailed paintings in which he now specialises. He works mainly in oils, taking up to two months to complete a painting – a similar amount of time being spent on research in the personal library of books and photographs he has built up over the years.

Barry's pictures have been reproduced in many forms, including collectors plates, book covers, greetings cards and jigsaw puzzles as well as fine art prints, which can now be found in many parts of the world. His paintings have also been featured in numerous railway publications and he has written several articles for *Artists and Illustrators' Magazine*. He has broadcast on BBC radio and appeared on both Anglia and Central television in connection with his work.

Sharing the Moment

Barry Freeman, GRA
Oils. 20in x 30in (508mm x 762mm)

Steam on the Met. 1994

G. Peter M. Green, GRA
Oils. 30in x 24in (762mm x 610mm)
Steam on the Met. was produced for poster publicity for London Underground Ltd. Metrovick Bo-Bo No. 12 Sarah Siddons pulls out of Rickmansworth on a London bound train, with ex-GWR 0-6-0 pannier tank with wagons and guards van in the bay road, Spring 1957.

PETER GREEN, GRA

Peter Green is known, at least in the London area, for the paintings he has produced over the past few years for London Underground's 'Steam on the Met' publicity, but his main occupation in recent times has been as illustrator for Union Railways Ltd (formerly a wholly owned subsidiary of British Rail) Channel Tunnel Rail Link project.

He was born in 1933 in Nantwich, near Crewe, Cheshire, to a railway modelling clergyman, which accounts for his long-life interest in railways, the LMS in particular. As an artist, early signs of talent were ignored and he entered a career in the silk industry, progressing eventually to selling and publicising Terylene with ICI Fibres Ltd, by whom he was moved to London over 30 years ago. He later went on to owning his own art shop in Harrow, which he gave up in 1987 to become a freelance artist, having developed his talent on his own account gradually over the previous 15 years.

The Spirits of St Pancras

G. Peter M. Green, GRA
Oils. 20in x 30in (510mm x 762mm)
The plan is for the new Channel Tunnel Rail Link to terminate at a somewhat altered and extended St Pancras station which will have direct connections with the East Coast, Midland and West Coast main lines, albeit with the present train shed and hotel buildings preserved. This fantasy scene shows, alongside the 'Eurostar' train, examples of arguably the most important locomotives which have served the terminus in the station's existence, viz. a Kirtley 2-4-0, a Johnson Single, a Deeley Compound, a Stanier 'Jubilee', a 'Peak' Class 45 diesel, an HST 125 and a 'Thameslink' EMU (Commissioned by Union Railways Ltd)

Euston Arrivals, c1960

G. Peter M. Green, GRA
Oils. 24in x 36in (610mm x 910mm)
Euston before modernisation and electrification; passengers disgorging from the 'Merseyside Express' brought into Platform 2 by Pacific No. 46201 Princess Elizabeth, *as another express arrives at Platform 1 behind Pacific No. 46244* King George VI – *father and daughter together.*

The LNWR Collection

G. Peter M. Green, GRA
Oils. 16in x 20in (406mm x 518mm)
The LNWR Collection – a group which includes, as well as books, timetables, post cards and a photograph, a mounted carriage transfer and the artist's Bing tin-plate toy train, which was his father's boyhood pride and joy.

London – Paris 10 Hours,
London – Paris 3 Hours

John Hardy
Acrylic. 8.75in x 12.25in
(220mm x 310mm)

JOHN HARDY

John Hardy has pursued a career in graphic design and advertising, including illustration, from the late 1950s, occasionally producing scenic pictures for his own interest.

Childhood evacuation with the family in a wartime location near the GWR main line, west of Taunton, awakened an early love of railways. Returning later to LNER territory in north east London, an interest in the rural and urban lines of the old Great Eastern developed.

Only in recent years however has he combined painting and railways, partly inspired by an art exhibition by the Guild promoting their book *To the Seaside*, seen at Foyles bookshop in London in 1990. This urged him to seek membership and gave the impetus to draw and paint the subject, with a confessed fondness for the pre-Grouping period, but not exclusively so.

Watercolour, acrylic, colour pencil and occasionally oil pastel are the mediums he favours. Local exhibitions have featured John's work in the vicinity of Broxbourne, Hertfordshire, where he lives.

JOHN HARRISON, GRA, ATD

Railways are the backcloth to his life. As a boy in the 'thirties the LMS was his daily scene – holidays, shopping, family visits: giant 'Scots' thundering through Wigan – ancient Webb tanks on motor trains to Rainford.

In the 'fifties he studied for National Diploma in Design and Art Teacher's Diploma at the Liverpool College of Art. Sketching involved frequent trips to the bustling docks, the Pier Head with trams and ferries, the Overhead Railway and the all-steam Lime Street station – all now history.

John began teaching within sight of Sutton Oak shed. He was soon running the school railway society and organising visits to the local shed, to Vulcan Foundry, with English Electric diesels under construction, and to Edge Hill depot where the party were photographed beside No. 46220 *Coronation*, with Type 4 diesel-electric No. D305 symbolically behind.

Latterly he was Head of Art in a large comprehensive school – but a quarter of the art room housed a model railway layout! Early retirement in 1988 enabled John to concentrate on railway art. John states, "my work is unashamedly nostalgic, seeking to recapture the men, machines and atmosphere of a departed way of life".

The Long Drag

John Harrison, GRA
Pen and Ink. 14in x 10in (350mm x 255mm)
Standard 2-10-0 on Dent Viaduct

LNWR Prince _on an Up Express at Preston_

John Harrison, GRA
Watercolour. 15in x 20.5in (385mm x 520mm)

Mist over the Mersey

John Harrison, GRA
Watercolour and Gouache. 14in x 21in (360mm x 535mm)
Runcorn Bridge in the 'thirties with Widnes Transporter Bridge behind.

Team Work

John Harrison, GRA
Pen and Wash. 16.5in x 21.5in (415mm x 540mm)

St Pancras Departure

Philip D. Hawkins, GRA
Oils. 16in x 20in (405mm x 510mm)
LMS-built Compound 4-4-0 No. 1097 makes a thunderous start from beneath the famous roof of
St Pancras at the head of a Manchester via Leicester express during the late 1920s. No. 1097
was built at Derby in 1925 and withdrawn from service by BR in 1956.

PHILIP D. HAWKINS, GRA

Maybe a childhood spent in Birmingham during the 1950s, surrounded by the sights and sounds of trains, is responsible for Philip's enduring passion for railways. This fascination and a natural artistic talent have combined to make his work highly sought after throughout the world. After graduating from Birmingham College of Art, he was employed in the railway industry as a technical illustrator at Metro-Cammell Ltd in Birmingham, and then as a press photographer and freelance illustrator through one or two further career changes until taking the plunge to concentrate on fine art.

Although steam locomotives, often in all their shop-soiled glory, have always featured heavily in Philip's work, nostalgia is by no means his only stock in trade! In recent years prestigious commissions from such companies as European Passenger Services (Eurostar), Brown & Root, Booz-Allen Ltd (contractors for the Docklands Light Railway), Railfreight and Freightliner are positive proof of his ability to transform what many would consider to be a clinical, lifeless subject into a finely observed and memorable image.

He has travelled extensively in pursuit of his quarry and drawings, photographs and notes made on these expeditions now prove to be an invaluable source of reference and add a very personal note to many of his paintings. Philip's work is published in many forms including fine art prints, greetings cards, calendars and in books and magazines. He was a Founder Member of the Guild of Railway Artists and is currently their President.

Twilight of the 20s

Philip D. Hawkins, GRA
Oils. 16in x 24in (405mm x 610mm)
Darkness falls over Bescot Yard as a pair of English Electric
Class 20s heaves coal hoppers bound for Ironbridge Power
Station out of the down yard during 1990.

Night Wolf

Philip D. Hawkins, GRA
Oils. 16in x 20in (405mm x 510mm)
Thompson Class A2/2 Pacific No. 60506 Wolf of Badenoch *lurking in the shed*
yard at New England, Peterborough waiting for a spell of night duty in 1960.
This locomotive was withdrawn from service in April 1961.

Freightliner 1995

Philip D. Hawkins, GRA
Oils. 14in x 21in (355mm x 533mm)
Birmingham Freightliner terminal plays host to Class 47s
Nos 47376 and 47301 during the autumn of 1995. The
painting was specially commissioned by Freightliner to
celebrate its 30th anniversary.

Millers Dale Junction

Carl Henderson, GRA
Oils. 24in x 37.5in (610mm x 950mm)

CARL HENDERSON, GRA

Carl Henderson was born in Sheffield in 1949. He spent his formative years on Doncaster station and scaling the wall outside 'The Plant'. After several career changes, including a spell working for BR in South London, Carl studied for his Degree in Fine Art at Liverpool. He spent many years teaching art but now paints full time.

Apart from exhibiting with the Guild, Carl has shown his work at Brunel University Gallery, Uxbridge, 1987; Hanover Gallery, Liverpool, 1991; Merkmal Gallery, Liverpool, 1991 and Quay Gallery, Exeter 1994.

Like O. Winston Link, who says he likes railways because "they go places", Carl is more interested in where, not how, trains go and how they shape, and are shaped by, the environment. Swimming against the tide of nostalgia Carl concentrates on the contemporary scene. He is thus able to rely on his own source material and looks towards the expanding future.

Cannon Street

Carl Henderson, GRA
Oils. 22in x 41in (558mm x 1041mm)

Grosvenor Bank

Carl Henderson, GRA
Oils. 36in x 55in (914mm x 1397mm)

Blackfriars

Carl Henderson, GRA
Oils. 22in x 41in (560mm x 1040mm)
King's Reach Tower, the home of Railway Magazine is
visible in the centre.

The Ash Man: Llanelli

John Hughes, GRA
Pen and Ink. 11in x 10in
(279mm x 254mm)
A member of a once-numerous body of
railwaymen doing a disagreeable job with
dignity and humour. Found wherever steam
engines were serviced, working mainly
outdoors, day or night, in all weathers. Their
working practices changed little in over a
hundred years but then neither did their
dedication to a job well done.

JOHN HUGHES, GRA.

Born in Birmingham in 1934, John Hughes had an interest in railways from an early age. Like countless hordes of small boys, he spent many happy hours perched on grassy embankments, peering over brick walls or pressed against iron railings, grubby paper and pencil stub in hand, recording the passage of the GWR's finest. These impressions of busy scenes witnessed in an age long past have endured ever since.

John is now retired, having spent most of his working life in the garage trade. He has raced power boats, model cars and long circuit karts, other long time interests include photography and modelling; in 1987 he decided to try his hand at painting.

Without the benefit of formal art training, reliance is placed on experience gained from 40 years of photography to assist in picture making and this probably explains the predilection for the graphic simplicity of monochrome images achieved with pen and ink. He also uses watercolour and lately has tried acrylics in a watercolour style. It's said that many photographers are frustrated painters, but John feels that he is more a frustrated photographer who paints.

Aberglaslyn Past

John Hughes, GRA
Acrylic. 12in x 17in (305mm x 432mm)
June 1940. In the South East of England, the fury, turmoil
and desperation that was the Battle of Britain; across the
Channel the Nazi horde poised to invade.
Two hundred and fifty miles to the north west, the Welsh
Highland Railway quietly moulders away, sunlight warms
the rusting rails, the stillness broken only by the gurgling
waters of the rocky Glaslyn.

Saltley Sunday Morning

John Hughes, GRA
Pen and Ink. 10in x 14in (254mm x 355mm)
In the halls of fiery giants, dark shapes loom balefully through the murk of steam and smoke,
vague ghostly figures move eerily in the gloom, a sulphurous fug lies acrid in the nostrils. The
fear of discovery in the dim light of this forbidden place mingles with the awe and excitement
of a possible bonanza. Such was the perilous path of the ardent young engine spotter.

On Shed: 'Mayflower'

John Hughes, GRA
Watercolour. 7in x 12in (178mm x 305mm)
She is cold now, energies spent, her pistons are still, but in the morning when the fire lighter
comes, then; then . . .

PETER INSOLE, GRA

Born in 1957 at Hainault, Essex, a mere stone's throw from the Underground station, it is reputed that his first artistic expression was copying the London Transport 'Target' logo, and by the age of ten, marine and animal subjects drawn from life brought some acclaim and several awards.

In 1968, the family move to a 'Beeching-axed' Suffolk town prompted the merging of his two main interests; any opportunity to ride on a train now included a sketch book and pencils!

On being presented with a tin of water-soluble crayons their colour and unique qualities led him to reject more traditional materials, preferring the challenge of developing the medium to fine-art standard over the following 26 years! Inspiration has always been the whole railway environment, particularly the journey; frequently being the sole occupant of a carriage and waiting or alighting at near-deserted stations, indeed, many of those early drawings are now providing an invaluable source for his current work.

Hurry up – the Shuttle's in!

Peter Insole, GRA
Crayon and Gouache.
14in x 11in
(355mm x 280mm)

67

On Time. Departure from Liverpool Street

Peter Insole, GRA
Crayon and Gouache. 14in x 12.75in (355mm x 324mm)

Essex after Sunset

Peter Insole, GRA
Crayon and Gouache.
10.25in x 15.25in
(260mm x 388mm)

Spandrels and Capitals

Peter Insole, GRA
Crayon and Gouache. 22.75in x 31.75in
(577mm x 806mm)

Glenfinnan Viaduct – West Highland Line

Brian C. Lancaster, GRA
Watercolour. 12.25in x 16.75in (311mm x 425mm)

Sun, Smoke and Steam,
Liverpool Street, London

Brian C. Lancaster, GRA
Watercolour. 12.5in x 16in
(311mm x 407mm)

BRIAN C. LANCASTER, FRSA, GRA

Being brought up in the 1930s in the heavily industrialised southern part of Lancashire with its extensive railway network, the sights, sounds, and smell of LMS and LNWR steam locomotives have left a lasting impression.

Brian has always drawn and painted – it ran in the family – and at the age of 15 he successfully gained a scholarship to Bolton College of Art, followed by a further three years at Southport Art College, studying graphic design, illustration and so on. During all of this time he painted, mainly in watercolours, and exhibited regularly at the Southport Annual Exhibitions.

After a spell of six years in Canada working in the design field, during which Brian was fortunate enough to witness the last regular North American steam workings, he returned to this country. Since then he has worked in his spare time in the steam preservation field, still with brush in hand, painting, lining and lettering. This led to many memorable footplate runs as a member of working parties.

It has always been the atmospheric qualities of railways that have gripped Brian, and hopefully this is reflected in his work, other subjects of great interest being industrial scenes, landscapes and architectural themes. He exhibits widely, particularly in the open London exhibitions, and has recently been elected to Associate Membership of the Royal Society of Marine Artists. For many years now Brian has worked as a self-employed illustrator (mostly architectural), equally divided with his painting career.

**Cotswold Country – The Old Station, Nailsworth,
Gloucestershire**

Brian C. Lancaster, GRA
Watercolour. 13in x 17.75in (330mm x 450mm)

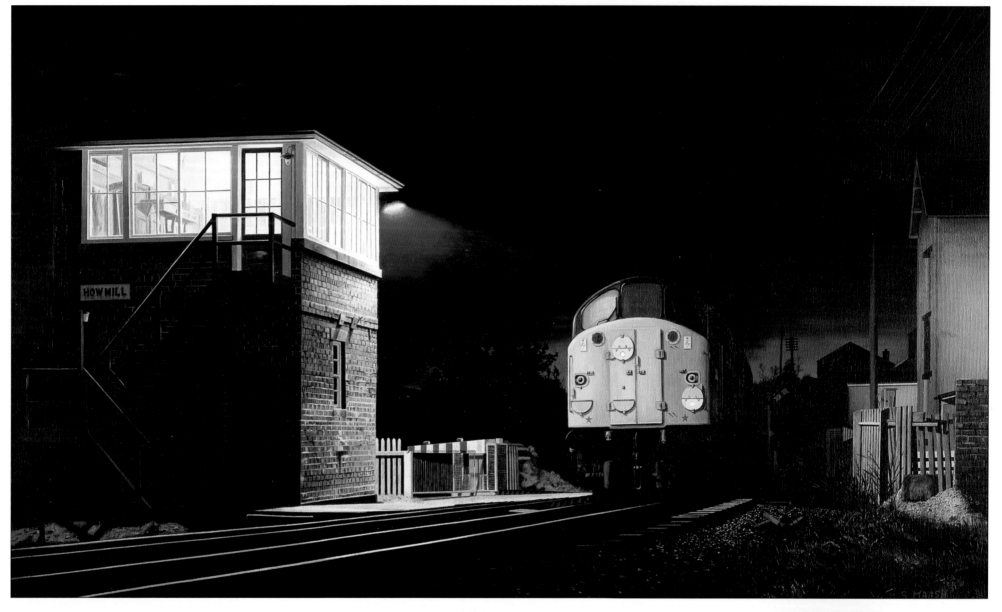

Night Freight at How Mill

Stuart Marsh
Oils. 18in x 30in
(460mm x 760mm)

An English Electric Type 4 (Class 40) locomotive heads a Kingmoor to Tyne Yard freight service past How Mill Crossing on the Carlisle–Newcastle line. The ex-NER signal box at How Mill became another statistic in the demise of mechanical signalling when closure took place on 22nd August 1989 after 114 years service and the crossing was converted to AHB operation. Of the tens of thousands of traditional signal boxes which once existed, there are now less than seven hundred mechanical installations still in use on the national network. There are still eleven such structures between Carlisle and Newcastle, nine of them NER design – but for how much longer?

STUART MARSH

Stuart Marsh attributes his deep interest in railways to his time spent as a boy, in and around the station at Culgaith, on the Settle–Carlisle line, where his grandfather was a signalman. "At that time", he says, "the railway scene was just a way of life to us and it is only with hindsight that I realise how privileged I was to be brought up amidst the sight, smell and sound of that classic line".

The memory of those early experiences have remained precious to him, and he feels that part of the fascination of painting is being able to create images of times that are lost, but which remain dear or important in our minds.

Indeed, his railway depictions are varied and he finds much interest in the modern railway

scene. Stuart has always loved painting, but it is only within the last ten years that he has turned to 'serious railway art' and that his work has reached a wider audience through publication and exhibitions.

The Lamp

Rob Milliken, GRA
Egg Tempera. 6in x 9in (150mm x 230mm)

ROB MILLIKEN, GRA

Rob Milliken was born in Harwich, Essex but spent much of his early years with his Dutch grandparents. He witnessed, during the post war years, the rebuilding of Rotterdam with its modern architecture and sculptures. His grandfather, who worked in a paint factory, would take Rob to the many art galleries in Holland and so the seed was sown.

Although he has no formal art training, what originally started as a hobby has now developed into a full-time occupation. Rob has a wide interest in subject matter although weathered textures, marine and transport are favoured themes. He has painted in a variety of mediums but these days concentrates on egg tempera, which he makes himself. He now lives and works in Nottingham.

Textures – Wood, Steel and Iron

Rob Milliken, GRA
Egg Tempera. 18in x 24in
(455mm x 610mm)

Three Below Zero

Rob Milliken, GRA
Egg Tempera. 7in x 10in (180mm x 260mm)

It Was

Rob Milliken, GRA
Mixed Media. 23in x 33in (580mm x 840mm)

Who you looking at then!

Richard Potts
Oils. 10in x 8in (254mm x 203mm)

RICHARD POTTS

Both 'Dick' Potts's grandfather and father were GWR drivers so it was inevitable that he would follow them. His father tried to divert his railway mania towards art school, but without success. So, after four years in the General Post Office and two years in the Royal Air Force he eventually started at Tyseley shed as a cleaner in 1949.

During 20 years at Tyseley, Dick worked on everything from pannier tanks to 'Kings' culminating with No. 6018 *King Henry VI* on the Stephenson Locomotive Society 'Last King' special from Birmingham to Swindon in 1963.

In 1969 he moved to Saltley as a driver where he worked on most types of diesel-electrics, from shunting engines to Class 60s, DMUs and HSTs. The most memorable was the honour of driving four Royal Trains.

Dick's railway experiences have been a constant inspiration for drawing and painting. He states that, "I could always draw from an early age but it wasn't until 1955 that I started to paint, and most of my commissions are for colleagues at work and friends".

Dick Potts finds great pleasure in sketching, particularly people and fishing boats, usually at St Ives in Cornwall where, with his wife Joy, they attend the St Ives School of Painting. It is here that he has his only tuition.

Dockland Sentinels

Laurence Roche, GRA
Acrylic. 14.5in x 17in (368mm x 431mm)

The Last Train from the Colliery

Laurence Roche, GRA
Acrylic. 15in x 18in (381mm x 457mm)

LAURENCE ROCHE, DA (EDIN), NDD, GRA

Among the many subjects that interest Laurence Roche are landscapes, seascapes and imagery of industry in general – past and present. These subjects are familiar to the artist and relate to personal experience. Furthermore, the theme of derelict and abandoned buildings which once saw human activity has always fascinated him, especially stations, signalboxes and other railway artifacts in the landscape – a legacy of the Beeching era.

This was the inspiration for his railway paintings which depict remnants still standing and remind us of a previous era. Other themes have since been developed – collieries, docklands, industrial railways and the imagery of the contemporary railway.

Laurence Roche was born in Goodwick, Pembrokeshire, studied at Swansea College of Art, and then at Edinburgh College of Art, where

he was awarded a post-graduate scholarship. He has exhibited widely, including several one-man shows. His work is included in private and corporate collections in the UK and abroad. His present position is as Company Artist to A. S. W. Holdings Plc, the Cardiff-based steel and wire producer.

Old Signal Box

Laurence Roche, GRA
Acrylic. 16in x 22in (457mm x 558mm)

A few lines between Preston and Carlisle

Laurence Roche, GRA
Acrylic. 18.5in x 21in (470mm x 533mm)

Constable Country

Malcolm Root, GRA
Oils. 20in x 24in (508mm x 609mm)
BR 'Britannia' Pacific No. 70003 John Bunyan *on an up train from East Anglia passing Dedham signal box in the late 1950s.*

Grit and Determination

Malcolm Root, GRA
Oils. 24in x 30in (610mm x 760mm)
The streamlined B17 class 4-6-0 No. 2859 East Anglian, *so named to work the train of the same name, climbing Bethnal Green Bank with the down train, prior to the Second World War.*

MALCOLM ROOT, GRA

Born in Colchester in 1950, Malcolm has lived in Halstead, north Essex, ever since. He left school at 16 and trained as a printing apprentice with a view to a career in design and typography. However, he left the printing trade in 1981 to become a full-time artist.

Although Malcolm had several small exhibitions in the early days, commissions followed on a regular basis so that he has always kept very busy. He was elected to Full Membership of the Guild of Railway Artists in 1983 and has had pictures hung in their exhibitions. Various paintings have also been published in books and magazines.

Malcolm Root's hobbies include football (but only as a spectator these days), cycling and local history. His greatest interest, however, is in mid-20th century transport and its impact on the ordinary person. Malcolm states that, "Trains and buses were used by the majority and independence only came to the lucky few who were fortunate enough to own a car. Travelling those days seemed to be more leisurely and more exciting – far removed from today's stressful and traffic-laden roads. Fortunately my town had its own station and I have fond memories of travelling by train, if only on a branch line".

At present Malcolm is busy painting for calendars, cards and prints as well as keeping up with commissioned work.

Snowdrift Assault

Malcolm Root, GRA
Oils. 18in x 24in (457mm x 610mm)
Two Class 2 Moguls, a BR Standard and an Ivatt, on
snow plough duty.

Lynton Evening

Malcolm Root, GRA
Oils. 16in x 20in (407mm x 508mm)
Lynton & Barnstaple Railway 2-6-2T No. 761 Taw arriving
at Lynton in the early 1930s.

82

On Time

Roy Schofield, GRA
Gouache. 14in x 22in
(355mm x 560mm)

ROY SCHOFIELD, GRA

Roy Schofield now lives in Surrey but his first 25 years were spent in and around the West Riding of Yorkshire. He studied illustration and graphic design at the Huddersfield School of Art.

His first job after National Service was in advertising and then, in 1958, he moved to London and joined the staff of the monthly magazine *Model Railway News* which, at that time, included the legendary J. N. Maskelyne. In 1963 he moved on to become Art Director in the Knightsbridge office of a Chicago-based publishing company. The opportunity was taken in 1967 to go freelance and this is still the situation today, working mainly as an illustrator on a range of educational projects for a publisher in Berlin.

Gouache and watercolour painting is very

much a spare-time occupation and allows him freedom to select and interpret the subject without any constraints that can accompany commissioned work.

An interest in railways has always been present and this is closely allied to his other hobby of model engineering. He can often be seen driving his 5in gauge steam locomotive on the club track at weekends.

The 5.59pm to Holmfirth

Roy Schofield, GRA
Gouache. 14.5in x 10.75in (360mm x 275mm)

The Ghosts of 56D (Mirfield MPD)

Roy Schofield, GRA
Mixed Media. 13.5in x 21.5in (345mm x 545mm)

Germiston Steam Sheds

David Shepherd, OBE, FRSA, FGRA
Oils. 29in x 63in (740mm x 1600mm)
"When I first went to this great Steam Depot in 1971, there must have been nearly 200 engines 'on shed' and the place was choking with smoke. Now, the place is almost deserted.
Little did I know when sketching for this painting in 1971 that I would aquire both a Class 7, on the left of the painting, and a 15F on the right, the former already back at home in England."

DAVID SHEPHERD, OBE, FRSA, FGRA

As a small boy, David collected books on Africa, and he had one ambition only, to become a game warden. His early career was, to quote his own words, "a series of disasters". After leaving school in 1949, he went to Kenya and was politely told that he was not wanted. Coming home again, David was faced with two choices; "to drive buses or starve as an artist". Rejected by the Slade School of Fine Art as having "no talent whatsoever", it was by good fortune that he met Robin Goodwin who took him under his wing and to whom he owes much of his success.

He started his career as an aviation artist and owes a great deal to the Royal Air Force. Whilst never having worn a uniform they recognised his work and started commissioning aviation paintings which involved flying all over the world with them. It was the Royal Air Force who flew David to Kenya in 1960 and this was the catalyst in his life. They commissioned his very first wildlife painting and, to quote David's own words, "I have never looked back".

David also has a passion for steam locomotives and in 1967 he purchased two main line steam locomotives, later named *Black Prince* and *The Green Knight* and founded the East Somerset Railway at Cranmore, Somerset, a registered charity and a fully operational steam railway. His latest venture is a 15F class locomotive, even larger than *Black Prince*, presented to him by South African Railways as a free gift. Fully restored, it is his intention to bring it back to Britain, to the East Somerset Railway, some time in the future.

David Shepherd was awarded an Honorary Degree of Fine Arts by the Pratt Institute in New York in 1971 and, in 1973, the Order of the Golden Ark by HRH The Prince of The Netherlands for his services to conservation. He was made a Member of Honour of the World Wide Fund for Nature in 1979 and received the Order of the British Empire for his services to

wildlife conservation. In 1986 David was elected a Fellow of the Royal Society of Arts and in 1988 President Kenneth Kaunda awarded him with the Order of Distinguished Service. He was made a Fellow of the Royal Geographical Society in 1989 and he was awarded an Honorary Doctorate of Science of Hatfield Polytechnic (now the University of Hertfordshire) in 1990.

David is married with four daughters and lives in Surrey.

GWR Relief Signalman

Philip Shepherd
Oils. 9.75in x 15in
(250mm x 380mm)

PHILIP SHEPHERD, RWS

Philip Shepherd is the son of a relief signalman. He currently resides at Wilmcote, Warwickshire. He studied fine art and illustration at Harrow and Birmingham Colleges of Art where he was privileged to receive the 'Classical' Art School Training without which he could never have become a professional artist. He has been a Technical, Advertising and Architectural Perspective Artist. Career highlights have been; election to the Royal Watercolour Society, awarded Bronze and Gold Medals at the Paris Salon, and wood engravings in the 'Fitzwilliam' and 'Whitworth' collections.

The love for GWR steam started with annual journeys from Paddington to Swansea behind 'Castles' in the 'thirties and playing under the railway bridge over the River Lliw at Pontlliw. However, it was the long-lived and interesting

working of the GWR push and pull auto trains that fascinated him.

Philip has a passion for signalling and Bewdley South box on the Severn Valley Railway in particular.

Long Marston Signal Box

Philip Shepherd
Oils. 12.25in x 17.75in (315mm x 450mm)

GWR 'Push and Pull', early 1930s

Philip Shepherd
Oils. 11.25in x 18.75in (290mm x 476mm)

Le Shuttle

Mike Turner, GRA
Oil Pastel. 17.5in x 25in (445mm x 630mm)
Le Shuttle, making rapid exit from the French portal of the Channel Tunnel.

Lewes, East Sussex, late '30s

Mike Turner, GRA
Watercolour and Gouache. 11in x 15.5in (285mm x 400m)
The low morning sun dramatises this scene as the Newhaven-Victoria Boat Train negotiates
the sharp curves through Lewes station behind a Brighton Atlantic. A U class 2-6-0 waits in
the adjacent platform, its driver and fireman relaxing before setting off for Hastings.

MIKE TURNER, GRA

Camden, Willesden, Cricklewood, evocative images for some, perhaps. This is where Mike Turner spent his childhood years, and while unappreciative of his surroundings at the time, it did influence his later aspirations in becoming a freelance illustrator.

Graduation from art college came in 1970/1 leading to a career in the field of graphic design, working for a small publishing company as a designer. Becoming disillusioned with lack of prospects, he quit and bought a touring bicycle, packed the panniers and headed for the Continent for a few months.

The return to Britain gave Mike another short spell of design experience at Goya International before accepting a post at the Sunday Times as an illustrator/designer. This was at a time where there was discontent with new working practices and so predictably he was made redundant.

Out of this maelstrom, Mike found himself in limited demand as a freelance illustrator. Work was featured occasionally in railway magazines. Prints and postcards appeared later, including a series depicting the years 1948/1988 on Britain's railways and events such as the Ashford 150 celebrations.

Mike Turner has since attained a reputation in South East England for his depictions of the Southern Railway scene. Continental scenes, especially Swiss, are specialities of his. He now resides in Hastings, East Sussex where sea, sky and landscape play an important part in influencing his continuing artistic creativity.

York

Mike Turner, GRA
Oil Pastel. 16in x 19.5in (410mm x 485mm)
York station and the electric InterCity era has arrived, 1991.

Storm Clouds over the Alps

Mike Turner, GRA
Watercolour and Gouache. 11in x 15.5in
(285mm x 400mm)
SBB Class RE4/4 descends the southern ramp of the
Gotthard at Giornico, Tincino, Southern Switzerland, with
a train for Milan.

L & Y

Stephen Warnes, GRA
Acrylic. 26in x 38in
(660mm x 965mm)
There was tremendous optimism in Accrington as the new century dawned. In a hundred years they had come from poverty and despair following the Enclosures Act, through the coming of the mills, exploitation – and then reform, and increasingly, a prosperity for all classes not known before. At the centre of it all was the Lancashire & Yorkshire Railway, feeder of its industries, mover of its people.

STEPHEN WARNES, GRA

Stephen Warnes was born in 1951 and grew up in North East Lancashire. He says, "Watching trains was an important part of my childhood. It gave me another world to escape into, and the images that come back now are tempered with a mixture of myth, magic, peace and emotion".

Stephen adds that, "Railways are a perfect example of the Saturnian world age, and for nearly two centuries have been at the heart of the social change brought about by industrialisation. My paintings try to reflect all of these things, and so often feature a more abstract and multi-layered approach."

Departure

Stephen Warnes, GRA
Acrylic. 30in x 36in (360mm x 915mm)
"In time I packed my cardboard suitcase, put it on a train,
Tied a little label to my days.
Didn't look back over shoulder, felt no loss along the way,
and went to find the things that would amaze."

JOE WILKES

Joe Wilkes was born in Walsall and some of his earliest recollections are being taken to see the turntable at Ryecroft sheds and lying in bed and listening to the sounds of the shunting at Bescot. This, he thinks, started his interest in railways.

He studied at Walsall College of Art and although pursuing a career as a structural draughtsman, painting was his first love. Some years after moving to Gloucestershire, the offer of early retirement gave Joe the opportunity to pursue his art career full time.

His fine art subjects include landscapes, aircraft and nature – some of which have been used for book covers and cards. Although not professing to be a railway buff, he finds locomotives the most challenging. Joe's favourite medium is oils but he also enjoys using watercolour and gouache.

Mixed Steam, Barrow Road Sheds

Joe Wilkes
Oils. 30in x 24in (762mm x 610mm)
A scene at the old LMS sheds, Bristol, around 1962 after being taken over by Western Region of British Railways. A GWR 0-6-2T, an LMS 'Black Five' and a Fowler 4F are the 'Mixed Steam'.

THE GUILD OF RAILWAY ARTISTS

THE Railway has been the subject for depiction by artists for a time even longer than that being celebrated by *Railway Magazine*. Claude Monet, J. M. W. Turner, W. P. Frith and John Cooke Bourne and others depicted the railways in their emerging years while Spencer Frederick Gore and Edward Hopper were two amongst many who depicted the heyday of the steam railway from the turn of the century to the 1940s. After the Second World War, the new era perhaps began with the emergence of paintings by Terence Cuneo, David Shepherd and Hamilton Ellis.

The Guild of Railway Artists is, when looking at the lifespan of *Railway Magazine*, a very young organisation, only just over half way through its teenage years. It was formed in October 1979 to provide a tangible link between artists depicting the heritage and the modern practices of the railway scene in its many facets. Its membership is spread over the length of Great Britain with some members residing beyond those shores in Europe and South Africa.

The membership includes both full-time artists and those who undertake their depictions in their leisure time. The mediums used by the artists cover a wide range – oils, acrylics and watercolour tend to predominate but other mediums such as pen and ink, pencil, pastel crayon, gouache and egg tempera also feature. Whilst the Guild exhibits only original works of art, a number of its members do have their work available as high quality fine art prints, in calendars and on greetings cards.

The Guild of Railway Artists congratulates *Railway Magazine* on its one-hundredth anniversary and is honoured to be part of their celebrations.

ENDPIECE

Finally, but by no means least – FRANK HODGES, the Chief Executive of the Guild of Railway Artists, or Mr G. R. A. as perhaps he should be known, because if it were not for his foresight and absolute dedication, there probably would not be a Guild of Railway Artists. Frank, one of the co-Founders, is not an artist and would not claim to be one, but his ability as an administrator is second to none.

Artists are not noted for their organisational skills, and with such a diverse group of individuals within the Guild of Railway Artists problems could arise, but not with Frank at the helm. Besides being an administrator he compiles, edits and publishes the quarterly GRA newsletter – the *Wheel and Palette*. Also, he takes on other mundane tasks others would not consider. You name it, Frank does it, always with undiminished fervour.

No one is indispensable – some go, others follow on – that is the way of things. But for the well-being of the Guild of Railway Artists it is hoped that Frank will be around for a long time to come, to continue the stalwart work he has done so well for so many years.

On behalf of all members of the Guild of Railway Artists, 'Thank you, Mr G. R. A.'

L.R. & P.D.H.

THE RAILWAY MAGAZINE ILLUSTRATED

This Number Commences a New Vol.

JANUARY 1899

CONTENTS

Illustrated Interviews:
No. XIX.—Mr. T. A. WILSON,
General Manager, Highland Railway.
The Glasgow Cable Railway
To the Sunny South by Railway
Some New Great Northern Engines
Electricity and the Safety of Railway
Travelling
Social Organisations among Railway
Employees
Saltcoats Station
&c., &c.

PRICE SIXPENCE

NO. 19 VOL. IV

79 & 80 TEMPLE CHAMBERS, TEMPLE AVENUE, LONDON E.C.

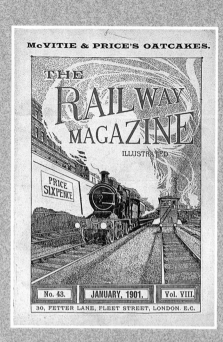

McVITIE & PRICE'S OATCAKES.

THE RAILWAY MAGAZINE ILLUSTRATED

PRICE SIXPENCE

No. 43. JANUARY, 1901. Vol. VIII.

30, FETTER LANE, FLEET STREET, LONDON. E.C.

NOVEL PRIZE COMPETITION. FOR PARTICULARS, SEE PAGE 432.

THE Railway Magazine. 6D

No. 77. NOVEMBER, 1903. Vol. XIII.

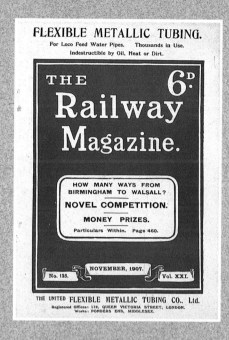

FLEXIBLE METALLIC TUBING.
For Loco Feed Water Pipes. Thousands in Use.
Indestructible by Oil, Heat or Dirt.

THE Railway Magazine. 6D

HOW MANY WAYS FROM BIRMINGHAM TO WALSALL?
NOVEL COMPETITION.
MONEY PRIZES.
Particulars Within. Page 460.

No. 125. NOVEMBER, 1907. Vol. XXI.

THE UNITED FLEXIBLE METALLIC TUBING CO., Ltd.
Registered Offices: 113, QUEEN VICTORIA STREET, LONDON.
Works: PONDERS END, MIDDLESEX.

FLEXIBLE METALLIC TUBING.
For Loco Feed Water Pipes. Thousands in Use.
Indestructible by Oil, Heat or Dirt.

THE Railway Magazine. 6D

This Number contains S.E. & C.R. Train Colour Plate.

SUMMER NUMBER ILLUSTRATED

JULY, 1915.

No. 217. Vol. XXXVII.

THE UNITED FLEXIBLE METALLIC TUBING CO., Ltd.
Registered Offices: 113, QUEEN VICTORIA STREET, LONDON.
Works: PONDERS END, MIDDLESEX.

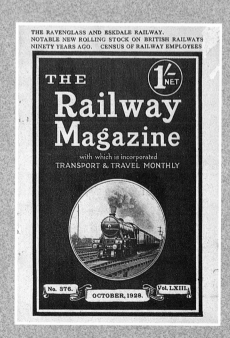

THE RAVENGLASS AND ESKDALE RAILWAY.
NOTABLE NEW ROLLING STOCK ON BRITISH RAILWAYS
NINETY YEARS AGO. CENSUS OF RAILWAY EMPLOYEES

THE Railway Magazine 1/- NET

with which is incorporated
TRANSPORT & TRAVEL MONTHLY

No. 376. OCTOBER, 1928. Vol. LXIII.

AFTER THIS—EVERY OTHER MONTH (see pp. 97 & 121)

THE Railway Magazine 1/- NET

No. 538. APRIL, 1942. Vol. 88

DIAMOND JUBILEE OF THE CITY & SOUTH LONDON RAILWAY
CANTERBURY & WHITSTABLE RAILWAY U.S.A. TRAIN SPEEDS

THE Railway Magazine 2/-

No. 598. FEBRUARY 1951 Vol. 97